A KNITTING
wrapsody

kristin omdahl

INTERWEAVE.
interweave.com

EDITOR Ann Budd

TECHNICAL EDITOR Therese Chynoweth

PHOTOGRAPHER Joe Hancock

PHOTO STYLIST Linda Takah, Carol Beaver

HAIR AND MAKEUP Kathy MacKay

ART DIRECTOR Liz Quan

COVER AND INTERIOR DESIGN Karla Baker

PRODUCTION Katherine Jackson

Interweave Press LLC
201 East Fourth Street
Loveland, CO 80537-5655 USA
interweave.com

Printed in China by Asia Pacific Offset, Ltd.

Library of Congress Cataloging-in-Publication Data

Omdahl, Kristin.

  A knitting wrapsody : innovative designs to wrap,
drape, and tie / Kristin Omdahl.

    p. cm.

  Includes bibliographical references and index.

  ISBN 978-1-59668-307-5 (pbk.)

  1. Knitting--Patterns. 2. Crocheting--Patterns. 3.
Scarves. 4. Shawls. I. Title.

TT825.O439 2010

746.43'2--dc22

                                    2010022845

10 9 8 7 6 5 4 3 2 1

dedication

To Marlon, my Shark Hunter.
I love you, sweetheart!

This book represents the talents and hard work
of many people. I wish to thank everyone at
Interweave for your support, especially Rebecca
Campbell, Jaime Guthals, Marilyn Murphy, and
Tricia Waddell. Thank you to Ann Budd for your
patience and brilliant attention to detail and
to Lauren Koestner for your gracious knitting
assistance. Thank you to my friends at Lantern
Moon for the beautiful handmade knitting
needles I used while knitting this collection.

contents

introduction

Convinced that all expectant mothers should make booties and blankets for their babies, I taught myself to knit and crochet while I was pregnant with my son. I was living overseas at the time and had extremely limited access to yarn, patterns, and education. Thanks to my mom, who sent supplies, I tackled both crafts with such gusto that by the time my son was born, I had themed layette sets for every day of the week (Rastafari, sailor, and angelic, just to name a few) and enough blankets for a whole nursery.

Knitting and crochet were in my blood, and I couldn't fathom the idea of quitting just because I didn't need to make any more baby items. I started to make shawls and thoroughly enjoyed making them in different shapes. Squares and rectangles were pretty easy to figure out based on the stitch and row gauge, but to design triangular and circular shawls, I combined some of my favorite equations from my ninth-grade geometry class with the stitch and row gauge. I always loved math in school and enjoy working out real-life problems with algebra and geometry. Combining math with knitting and crochet was a spectacular "aha" moment for me. This was something I wanted to seriously explore.

I needed to work after my son was born, but I desperately wanted to stay at home with him. I had dreamed of making a living through my knitting and crochet and decided to make it happen. I sold shawls to boutiques for a while, created my first website (www.StyledbyKristin.com), and started writing patterns. My first published pattern was for a knitted sweater, the second was for a crocheted sweater. I wrote my first book *Wrapped in Crochet: Scarves, Wraps & Shawls* a few years ago. My follow-up book *Crochet so Fine: Exquisite Designs with Fine Yarns* came next.

I am thrilled to now introduce *A Knitting Wrapsody*, my first knitting book. Here, you'll find a collection of knit scarves, wraps, and shawls, with a focus on accessories that are wrapped and tied. Every project is knitted, but much of the aesthetic is inspired by crochet. For me, knitting and crochet are intertwined and this collection draws inspiration from the geometry, motifs, and techniques of crochet, but in the medium of knitting.

Some of the techniques are quite unusual. You may find it helpful to watch the enclosed DVD to see some of them demonstrated before you cast on for a project. Whether you are learning new techniques, trying something different, or relaxing with comforting, familiar stitches, remember to breathe and have fun!

Kristin

scarves

◄▷

This chapter highlights a variety of my experiments in knitting design with a collection of scarves that are quick and easy, but each has a surprise twist. The cut-out flower design in Lucky Clover (page 20) is inspired by crochet flower stitch patterns but is created through an unusual variation of cast-ons and bind-off buttonholes. The generous ruffled edge in Melange (page 26) is achieved with extreme variances in gauge, not increases and decreases as might be expected. Reversible cables and doubled buttons on both sides of one edge of Echo (page 30) make a quick project that can be worn four different ways. The I Do lace scarf (page 10) is an illusion of offset diamond motifs knitted in one continuous fabric. The ruffles are unusual, yet incredibly east to knit, in the Nerina Scarf (page 16). Thanks to the addition of laces (tied with my favorite fishing knots), this scarf can also be worn as a cowl or capelet.

i do
DIAMOND LACE SCARF

Although this design suggests separate motifs that are joined together, it is knitted in a single piece. The geometric circle-in-a-square motif forms a diamond, which brings to my mind a large diamond solitaire engagement ring. The squares are worked from tip to tip in diamond formation, and the sides are framed by a modified half-square and half-circle. This geometric pattern is completely reversible and requires just one skein of yarn. For a longer scarf, double the yardage and number of row repeats; for a beautiful wrap, double the yardage and number of stitches per row. With four skeins, you could double both the width and length for a luxurious shawl.

MATERIALS

FINISHED SIZE
About 10" (25.5 cm) wide and 52" (132 cm) long.

YARN
Fingering weight (#1 Super Fine).

shown here: Buffalo Gold Lux (45% premium bison down, 20% fine cashmere, 20% mulberry silk, 15% Tencel; 330 yd [302 m]/40 g): #12 Huckleberry, 1 skein.

NEEDLES
Size U.S. 6 (4 mm). *Adjust needle size if necessary to obtain the correct gauge.*

NOTIONS
Markers (m); tapestry needle.

GAUGE
25 stitches and 18 rows = 4" (10 cm) in lace pattern, blocked.

Dec4 (5 sts dec'd to 1 st)

Sl 3 sts knitwise, k2tog, p3sso—1 st rem.

R-inc (1 st inc'd to 2 sts)

Knit into the st below the first st on the left needle, then knit the first st on the left needle—1 st inc'd.

L-inc (1 st inc'd to 2 sts)

Knit the first st on the left needle, then knit into the back of the stitch in the row below the stitch just knitted—1 st inc'd.

Scarf

CO 3 sts. Knit 1 (WS) row. Knitting every WS row (not shown on chart), work Rows 2–106 of Diamond Lace chart (see page 14), then rep Rows 56–106 once, then rep Rows 56–104 once again, then work Rows 108–158 once, ending with a WS row—3 sts rem.

Finishing

Weave in loose ends. Wet-block and pin to finished measurements. Let air-dry completely before removing pins.

Wrap-3

The wrap-3 stitch gives great contrast to the following row of lace increases that amplifies the growth of the circle motif. Without it, this lace pattern would have more of a pointed diamond shape.

Bring yarn to front, sl 3 sts purlwise (**Figure 1**), bring yarn to back, sl the same 3 sts back onto left-hand needle (**Figure 2**), then knit the same 3 sts.

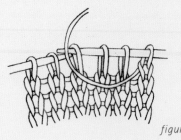

figure 1

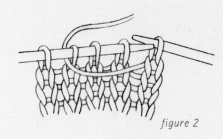

figure 2

Each lace medallion in this scarf is framed with garter-stitch diamonds. There are a few unusual stitches used to create the perfectly circular lace medallions, but they are easily learned. If you are new to lace, try working this scarf first with larger needles and thicker yarn. The modified scarf will be bigger, and you will get two looks from the same pattern!

I Do

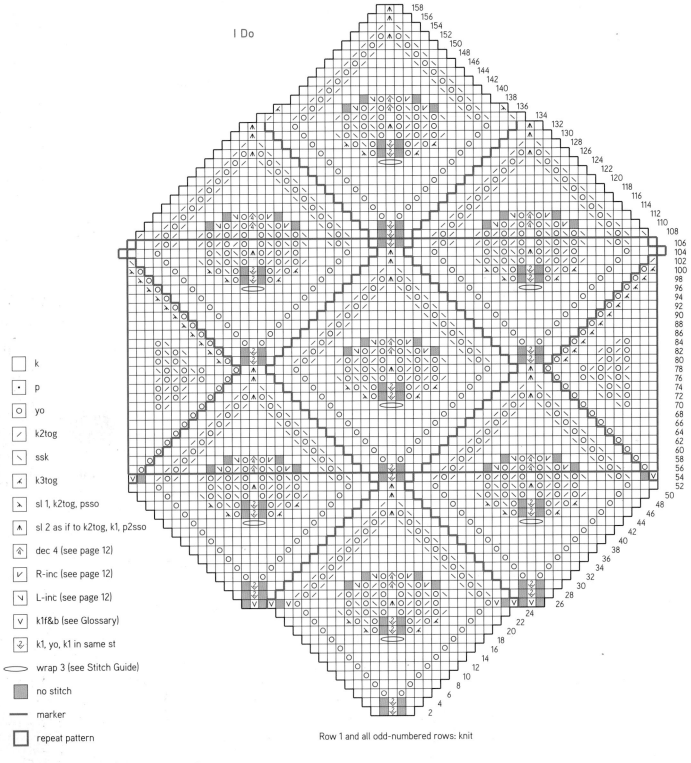

k

· p

○ yo

╱ k2tog

╲ ssk

⋏ k3tog

⋋ sl 1, k2tog, psso

⋀ sl 2 as if to k2tog, k1, p2sso

⬆ dec 4 (see page 12)

V R-inc (see page 12)

⋁ L-inc (see page 12)

V k1f&b (see Glossary)

⟱ k1, yo, k1 in same st

⬭ wrap 3 (see Stitch Guide)

▨ no stitch

— marker

▢ repeat pattern

Row 1 and all odd-numbered rows: knit

nerina
RUCHED AND RUFFLED SCARF

This ruffled scarf is cinched with a pair of satin cord drawstrings that are tied with double uni-knots (one of my favorite types of fishing knots). The scarf is knitted in a reversible ribbed pattern with regularly spaced short-rows to produce the ruffles along the edges. The holes created by the short-row turns provide eyelets through which the satin cords are threaded. Depending on how tightly the drawstrings are cinched, the ruffles contract from open and loose to a dense, thick mass. Tie it loosely around your shoulders for a little capelet, tighten the drawstrings a bit for soft ruffles, or cinch them all the way for a heavily ruffled collar or cowl.

NOTES

- Do not wrap stitches when working the short-row turns; the holes are used for lacing the drawstring.
- See the accompanying DVD for a demonstration on working the short-row shaping.

MATERIALS

FINISHED SIZE
About 7½" (19 cm) wide and 54" (137 cm) long, ungathered.

YARN
Worsted weight (#4 Medium).

shown here: Blue Sky Alpaca Suri Merino (60% baby suri alpaca, 40% merino; 164 yd [150 m]/100 g): #419 Crimson, 2 skeins.

NEEDLES
Size U.S. 6 (4 mm). *Adjust needle size if necessary to obtain the correct gauge.*

NOTIONS
12 yd (11 m) ⅛" (3 mm) diameter satin cord; tapestry needle.

GAUGE
19 stitches and 33 rows = 4" (10 cm) in ruched pattern.

◀▶◀▶◀▶◀▶ *The rippling texture in this two-row pattern is beautiful when flat but pops into luxurious ruffles when cinched with the drawstrings. The short-rows may be a bit of challenge at the beginning, but you'll enjoy watching the ruffles emerge from the technique.*

Scarf

CO 36 sts.

SET-UP ROW: Knit.

ROWS 1 AND 3: P10, turn, k10, turn, p10, *k3, p10, turn, k10, turn, p10; rep from * once more.

ROWS 2 AND 4: Knit.

ROWS 5 AND 7: K10, turn, p10, turn, k10, *k3, k10, turn, p10, turn, k10; rep from * once more.

ROWS 6 AND 8: P10, *k3, p10; rep from * once.

Rep Rows 1–8 until scarf measures about 54" (137 cm) from CO. Loosely BO all sts.

Finishing

Weave in loose ends. Wet-block and pin to finished measurements. Let air-dry completely before removing pins.

Ties

Cut the satin cord into two 6 yd (5.5 m) lengths. Beg at one short edge, weave one cord in and out of the holes formed by the short-row turns on one side of the garter-st center, across the middle ruffle edge, and back down the other side in a U path as shown in Threading Diagram on page 19. Tie the ends of the cord in a uni-knot as described in box at right. Beg at the other short edge, weave the other cord in and out of the rem short-row holes.

Double Uni-Knot

The double uni-knot, used for tying flies, is surprisingly easy to make. One of the best features is that you can cut the tails right next to the knot.

Lay the two strands parallel to each other on a flat surface. Bring the tail of the lower strand back on itself to make a loop, then cross it over the upper strand (**Figure 1**). Wrap the short end around both strands three times, bringing it to through to the front of the loop on the third wrap (**Figure 2**). Pull on both ends of this strand to tighten the knot (**Figure 3**). Wrap the upper strand in the same manner (**Figure 4**), then tighten both ends (**Figure 5**).

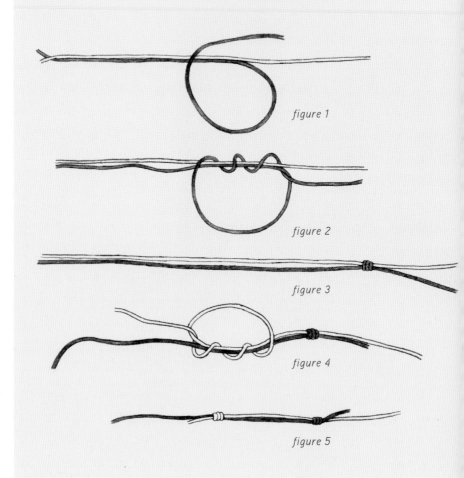

figure 1

figure 2

figure 3

figure 4

figure 5

Threading Diagram

○ hole

▬ first cord, threaded over top

▬ first cord, threaded under

▬ second cord, threaded over top

▬ second cord, threaded under

∅∅ uni-knot

lucky clover

REVERSIBLE SCARF WITH FOUR-PETAL CUTOUTS

For this project, I challenged myself to create a crochet-inspired floral design using cutouts, or negative space. The scarf begins with a picot cast-on, then is worked lengthwise in a reversible seed-stitch pattern punctuated with four-petal, clover-shaped openings, and ends with a pretty picot bind-off. To unify the picots for a full, symmetrical border, I added picots to the short side edges every few rows to match the picots on the cast-on and bind-off edges. The entire scarf is only 32 rows long! Worked in a chunky yarn, you can easily make one for a gift—or for yourself—this weekend.

MATERIALS

FINISHED SIZE
About 7½" (19 cm) wide and 57" (145 cm) long.

YARN
Chunky weight (#5 Bulky).

shown here: Malabrigo Yarns Chunky Merino (100% merino; 100 yd [91 m]/100 g): #37 Lettuce, 2 skeins.

NEEDLES
Size U.S. 10 (6.0 mm): 32" (80 cm) circular (cir). *Adjust needle size if necessary to obtain the correct gauge.*

NOTIONS
Bobbins (optional); tapestry needle.

GAUGE
10 stitches and 21 rows = 4" (10 cm) in seed-stitch pattern, after blocking.

Picot Cast-On (PCO)

Use the knitted method (see Glossary) to CO 3 sts, k2, lift the first st over the second st and off the needle (**Figure 1**), k1, lift the first st over the second st and off the needle (**Figure 2**), return remaining st to left needle tip (**Figure 3**) to cast on 1 st.

Scarf

Using the picot method (see at right), CO 142 sts as foll: *Use the knitted method (see Glossary) to CO 6 sts, BO 2 sts; rep from * 34 more times—142 sts.

ROWS 1 AND 3: *K1, p1; rep from *.

ROWS 2 AND 4: *P1, k1; rep from *.

ROW 5: 3-st picot (see page 23), *p1, k1; rep from * to last st, p1.

ROW 6: 3-st picot, *k1, p1; rep from * to last st, k1.

ROW 7: [K1, p1] 3 times, k1, *[p1, k1] 7 times, [yo] 2 times; rep from * 7 more times, [p1, k1] 11 times, p1—158 sts.

ROW 8: [P1, k1] 11 times, *p2tog (next st and first loop of double yo of prev row), k2tog (second loop of double yo and next st), [p1, k1] 6 times; rep from * 7 more times, [p1, k1] 4 times—142 sts.

ROWS 9 AND 10: Rep Rows 1 and 2.

ROW 11: 3-st picot, [p1, k1] 3 times, *[p1, k1] 3 times, BO 2 sts, [p1, k1] 3 times; rep from * 8 more times, [p1, k1] 4 times, p1—124 sts.

Openwork Clover

ROW 12: 3-st picot, [k1, p1] 7 times, turn work— 116 sts unworked.

ROWS 13, 14, AND 15: [P1, k1] 7 times, p1.

Leaving ball of yarn attached to Row 15, leave sts just worked on needle. Join a strand of yarn about 66" (167.5 cm) long to the next BO-2 gap for the next section. Work as foll:

ROWS 12 AND 14: [K1, p1] 6 times, turn.

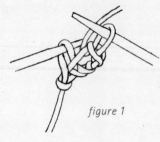

figure 1

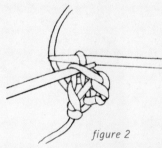

figure 2

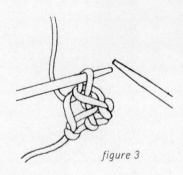

figure 3

Picot Bind-Off (PBO)

*Use knitted method (see Glossary) to CO 2 sts, k2, lift first st over second st and off the needle (**Figure 1**), k1, lift first st over second st and off the needle (**Figure 2**) to bind off 1 st; rep from * for desired number of sts.

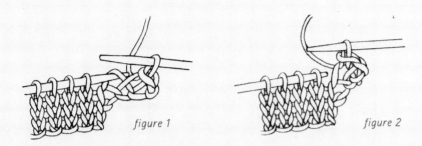

figure 1   *figure 2*

3-Stitch Picot

Use knitted method (see Glossary) to CO 3 sts, k2, lift first st over second st and off needle (**Figure 1**), k1, lift first st over second st and off needle (**Figure 2**), knit first st of scarf, lift first st on right needle tip over this st and off needle to bind off 1 (the third) st (**Figure 3**).

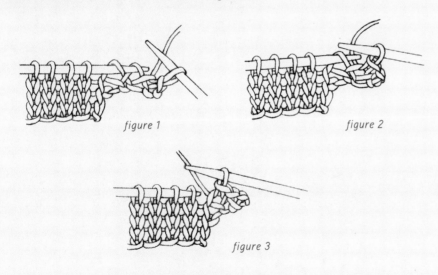

figure 1   *figure 2*

figure 3

ROWS 13 AND 15: [P1, k1] 6 times, turn.

Rep Rows 12–15 for each of the next six 12-st sections, leaving sts on needle after working each section. For the last section, join a strand of yarn about 72" (183 cm) long and work as foll:

ROWS 12–15: [K1, p1] 6 times, k1.

Join all sections as foll:

ROW 16: Beg with the first section worked, [p1, k1] 7 times, p1, *use the knitted method to CO 2 sts, [k1, p1] 6 times; rep from * 8 more times, k1—142 sts.

ROW 17: 3-st picot, [p1, k1] 4 times, *BO 10 sts, [p1, k1] 2 times; rep from * 8 times, [p1, k1] 3 times, p1—52 sts.

ROW 18: 3-st picot, [k1, p1] 5 times, *use the knitted method to CO 4 sts, [yo, pick up and knit 1 st in hole above 2 CO sts from Row 16] 4 times, use the knitted method to CO 4 sts, [k1, p1] 2 times; rep from * 8 more times, [k1, p1] 2 times, p1—187 sts.

ROW 19: [K1, p1] 3 times, k1, *[p1, k1] 3 times, k3tog, k4tog, pass first st on right needle tip over second st and off needle to BO 1, p1, pass first st on right needle tip over second st and off needle (5 sts dec'd and 2 sts BO), [k1, p1] 2 times, k1; rep from * 8 more times, [k1, p1] 4 times, p1—124 sts.

ROW 20: [P1, k1] 7 times, p1, turn work—109 sts unworked.

ROWS 21–23: [K1, p1] 7 times, p1.

Do not fasten off. Cut yarn, leaving a 6" (15 cm) tail. Wind tail in a bobbin and leave sts just worked on needle. For the next section, join a strand of yarn about 66" (167.5 cm) long to next BO-2 gap. Work as foll:

ROWS 20 AND 22: [K2, p2] 6 times, turn.

ROWS 21 AND 23: [P2, k2] 6 times.

Rep Rows 20–23 for each of the next six 12-st sections, leaving sts on needle after working

each section. For the last section, join a strand of yarn about 72" (183 cm) long and work as foll:

ROWS 20–22: [K1, p1] 6 times, k1.

ROW 23: 3-st picot, [p1, k1] 6 times.

ROW 24: Beg with the first section worked, 3-st picot, [k1, p1] 7 times, *use the knitted method to CO 2 sts, [k1, p1] 6 times; rep from * 8 more times, k1—142 sts.

ROWS 25 AND 26: Rep Rows 1 and 2.

ROW 27: Rep Row 7.

ROW 28: Rep Row 8.

ROWS 29 AND 31: *K1, p1; rep from *.

ROWS 30 AND 32: *P1, k1; rep from *—piece measures about 6¾" (17 cm) from CO.

Using the picot method, BO all foll: BO 2 sts, *use the knitted method to CO 2 sts, BO 6 sts; rep from *.

Finishing

Weave in loose ends, winding ends twice around picked-up sts at center of each clover before weaving them in. Wet-block and pin to finished measurements. Let air-dry completely before removing pins.

melange
CROCHET-LOOK SCARF

Again inspired by crochet, the main section of this scarf is worked in a knitted stitch pattern that has the beautiful geometry of an offset crochet shell motif. The shell shapes are achieved through elongated drop stitches combined with quadruple decreases. The stitch pattern is repeated every four rows, but every other repeat is offset so that the motifs stack on top of one another brick-fashion. The edging, worked at a much looser gauge than the body of the scarf, resembles a series of crochet chains (and is just as easy to work) that creates a generous ruffle at each end.

NOTES

- To soften the yarn, wind it into balls a couple of times—the more the yarn is handled, the softer it will become. Wash the scarf a few times to soften up the yarn even more.
- See the accompanying DVD for a demonstration on working the chain-2 bind-off.

MATERIALS

FINISHED SIZE
About 6" (15 cm) wide and 79" (201 cm) long with two 7" (18 cm) ruffles.

YARN
Sportweight (#2 Fine).

shown here: Louet North America Euroflax Sport (100% wet-spun linen; 270 yd [247 m]/100 g): #27 crabapple, 1 skein (with very little left over).

NEEDLES
Size U.S. 5 (3.75 mm). *Adjust needle size if necessary to obtain the correct gauge.*

NOTIONS
Contrasting cotton waste yarn for provisional cast-on; tapestry needle.

GAUGE
21 stitches and 13 rows = 4" (10 cm) in pattern stitch, after blocking.

Scarf

With waste yarn and using a provisional method (see Glossary), CO 33 sts.

ROW 1: (WS) K1, *yo, k1; rep from * to last st, k1.

ROW 2: Knit, dropping all yo's of previous row off of needle—33 sts.

ROW 3: K1, k3tog, *[yo] 2 times, k1, [yo] 2 times, sl 2, k3tog, p2sso; rep from * to last 5 sts, [yo] 2 times, k1, [yo] 2 times, k3tog, k1.

ROW 4: K1, *k1, knit into front and back of double yo; rep from * to last 2 sts, k2.

ROWS 5 AND 6: Rep Rows 1 and 2.

ROW 7: K1, *k1, [yo] 2 times, sl 2, k3tog, p2sso, [yo] 2 times; rep from * to last 2 sts, k2.

ROW 8: Rep Row 4.

Rep Rows 1–8 until piece measures about 64" (162.5 cm) from CO, ending with Row 8.

NEXT ROW: Knit, working into the front and back of each double yo, and increasing 1 extra st anywhere along the row—34 sts.

First Ruffle

*K2, [yo, pull the last st over the yo] 4 times; rep from * to end of row.

Rep this row 7 more times.

Using the chain-2 method (see at right), BO all sts.

Chain-2 Bind-Off

This bind-off technique is inspired by the super stretchy ruffle stitch pattern in the scarf. The chain-2 is knitted between each bound-off stitch and complements the ruffle stitch nicely. It would also make a pretty design element in any project requiring an extremely stretchy bind-off. The chain loops are easy to pin out and block to form a pretty scallop edge.

*BO 1 st (**Figure 1**), [yo (**Figure 2**), pull the first st over the yo as if to BO] 3 times to form a chain (**Figure 3**)—1 st bound off; rep from * for desired number of sts.

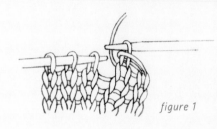

figure 1

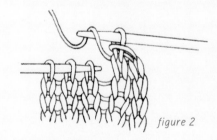

figure 2

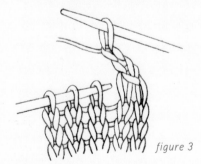

figure 3

Second Ruffle

Carefully remove waste yarn from provisional CO and place 33 exposed sts on needle. Work as for first ruffle.

Finishing

Weave in loose ends. Wet-block and pin to finished measurements. Let air-dry completely before removing pins.

echo
REVERSIBLE DROP-STITCH MOBIUS

Worked in a reversible fabric, both the right and wrong sides of this mobius wrap look the same. To showcase the unusual texture of the beautiful yarn, I incorporated dropped stitches—which form simple un-stitched yarn and ensure a pretty drape. For versatility, I worked this project in a flat piece and added buttons on the right and wrong sides so that it could be fastened with or without the mobius twist. Twisted and secured, you've got a mobius. Straight and secured with one or two buttons, you've got a capelet. Wrapped twice around the neck and secured with one or two buttons, you've got a cowl. Flat and gorgeous all on its own, you've got a reversible scarf!

NOTE

- See the accompanying DVD for a demon-stration on working the chain-2 bind-off.

MATERIALS

FINISHED SIZE
About 10" (25.5 cm) wide and 38" (96.5 cm) long, relaxed after blocking.

Note: The ribbing and dropped stitches make this fabric very stretchy.

YARN
Chunky weight (#5 Bulky).

shown here: Tahki Stacy Charles Loop-D-Loop Granite (95% merino, 5% nylon; 55 yd [50 m]/50 g): #002 Mahogany, 4 balls.

NEEDLES
Size U.S. 13 (9 mm): 24" (60 cm) circular (cir). *Adjust needle size if nec-essary to obtain the correct gauge.*

NOTIONS
Cable needle (cn); tapestry needle; six 1" (2.5 cm) buttons (buttons shown are JHB #1670 available at www.JoAnn.com).

GAUGE
12-stitch cable = 2½" (6.5 cm) wide; dropped stitch = 1¼" (3.2 cm) wide.

Note: This fabric is very stretchy; exact gauge is not critical.

2/2LC (worked over 8 sts)

Slip 4 sts onto cn and hold in front of work, work next 4 sts as [k1, p1] 2 times, work 4 sts from cn as [k1, p1] 2 times.

2/2RC (worked over 8 sts)

Slip 4 sts onto cn and hold in back of work, work next 4 sts as [k1, p1] 2 times, work 4 sts from ch as [k1, p1] 2 times.

Scarf

CO 38 sts.

ROW 1: [K1, p1] 6 times, *k1, [k1, p1] 6 times; rep from * once.

ROWS 2, 3, AND 4: Rep Row 1.

ROW 5: 2/2LC (see Stitch Guide), [k1, p1] 2 times, *k1, 2/2LC, [k1, p1] 2 times; rep from * once.

ROWS 6–10: Rep Row 1.

ROW 11: [K1, p1] 2 times, 2/2RC (see Stitch Guide), *k1, [k1, p1] 2 times, 2/2RC; rep from * once.

ROW 12: Rep Row 1.

Rep Rows 1–12 ten more times, then rep Rows 1 and 2 once more—piece measures about 37" (94 cm) from CO.

NEXT ROW: (Buttonhole row) [K1, p1] 2 times, k1, BO 2 sts, p1, [k1, p1] 2 times, *k1, [k1, p1] 2 times, k1, BO 2 sts, p1, [k1, p1] 2 times; rep from * once.

NEXT ROW: [K1, p1] 2 times, [(k1, p1) in next st] 2 times, [k1, p1] 2 times, *k1, [k1, p1] 2 times, [(k1, p1) in next st] 2 times, [k1, p1] 2 times.

NEXT ROW: Rep Row 5.

NEXT ROW: Rep Row 1.

Loosely BO 12 sts in patt, draw yarn through st on right-hand needle to fasten off but do not cut yarn, k1, BO next 12 sts in patt, draw yarn through last st on right-hand needle to fasten off but do not cut yarn, k1, BO rem 12 sts in patt and draw yarn through last st and fasten off. Drop rem 2 sts from right needle and ravel to CO edge.

Finishing

Sew three sets of two buttons tog (one on RS and one on WS of fabric, opposite buttonholes) 1" (2.5 cm) in from edge and centered in each of the cable panels. Wrap yarn around the base of each button to form a shank as shown at right.

Weave in loose ends. Wet-block and pin to finished measurements. Let air-dry completely before removing pins.

For a larger, luxurious wrap, double the width and length: Cast on 64 stitches (a multiple of 13 stitches plus 12) and knit until the piece is 72" (183 cm) long. But plan for four times as much yarn—880 yards (805 meters)—if you do.

Button Shank Diagram

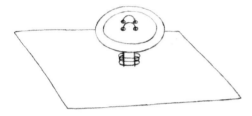

wraps

I think of wraps as a transition between shawls and sweaters. They are more contoured than a shawl but less complicated in shaping than a sweater. As a bonus, shawls can often be worn in multiple ways. In this chapter, I provide two cardi-wraps, a corset-laced cape, a shrug, and a ruana. While I often get my ideas from nature, this chapter highlights a variety of surprising sources. Rings of Cables (page 66) was inspired by hearing the song "Ring of Fire" sung by Adam Lambert; Tree of Life (page 58) was inspired by a painting by Tim Parrish; Anouk (page 36) honors a character in the movie *Chocolat*; Summit (page 72) came to me as I was thinking about a fantasy ski vacation; and Infinity (page 48) represents my quest for the perfect yarn to accentuate the shape and direction of the infinity motif with just the right amount of color striping and texture. Sand Dollar (page 42) is rightfully named for the sea urchin I intended to re-create in the medium of knitting.

anouk

LEATHER-LACED
RAGLAN CAPE

Named for a character in *Chocolat*, one of my favorite movies, this cape was an experiment in design. It is shaped with a traditional raglan yoke, but I separated the front section from the sides (the "sleeves"), added buttonholes in the diagonal edges of the raglan edges, and laced the seams like a corset from the neck to the elbow. The raglan-shaped yoke flatters the upper body and the open sides allow for free range of motion. The combination of Ultrasuede tape ribbon with fine merino wool gives this cape a casual rustic feel that would dress up tall boots, skinny jeans, and a turtleneck sweater.

MATERIALS

FINISHED SIZE
About 24" (61 cm) long.

YARN
DK weight (#3 Light).

shown here: Filatura Di Crosa Zara (100% superwash merino; 136 yd [125 m]/50 g): #1901 Brick, 12 balls.

NEEDLES
Size U.S. 6 (4 mm): 24" (60 cm) circular. *Adjust needle size if necessary to obtain the correct gauge.*

NOTIONS
Markers (m); 4 yd (3.6 m) of ¾" (2 cm) wide Ultrasuede tape (tape shown is item #31662, 20MM, in Coffee from www.mjtrim.com).

GAUGE
24 stitches and 26 rows = 4" (10 cm) in rib pattern, after blocking.

Front

CO 34 sts.

ROW 1: (WS) K1, p1, k1, [p4, k4] 3 times, p4, k1, p1, k1.

ROW 2: K1, p1, k1, [k4, p4] 3 times, k4, k1, p1, k1.

ROWS 3–8: Rep Rows 1 and 2 three more times.

ROW 9: K1, p1, k1, [yo] 2 times, work the sts as they appear (knit the knits; purl the purls) to last 3 sts, [yo] 2 times, k1, p1, k1—38 sts.

ROW 10: K1, p1, k2tog (next st and first wrap of double yo), p1 (second wrap of double yo), work the sts as they appear to next double yo, p1 (first wrap of double yo), k2tog (second wrap of double yo and next st), p1, k1—36 sts rem.

ROW 11: K1, p1, k1, M1R (see Glossary), work the sts as they appear to last 3 sts, M1L (see Glossary), k1, p1, k1—2 sts inc'd.

Working new sts into patt as they become available (after 4 consecutive knit increases, make sure the next 4 consecutive increases are purled), cont as foll:

ROWS 12, 14, AND 16: K1, p1, k1, work the sts as they appear to last 3 sts, k1, p1, k1.

ROW 13: Rep Row 11—40 sts.

ROW 15: Rep Row 11—42 sts.

ROWS 17–66: Rep Rows 9–16 six more times, then work Rows 9 and 10 once more—92 sts after Row 66.

ROWS 67–80: Rep Rows 11 and 12 seven more times—106 sts after Row 80.

Work even until piece measures about 23¼" (59 cm) from CO.

NEXT ROW: *K1, p1; rep from * to last st, k1.

Rep the last row 3 more times. Loosely BO all sts in patt.

Back

CO 74 sts.

ROW 1: (WS) K1, p1, k1, [k4, p4] 2 times, place marker (pm), k4, pm, [p4, k4] 3 times, p4, pm, k4, pm, [p4, k4] 2 times, k1, p1, k1.

ROW 2: K1, p1, k1, [p4, k4] 2 times, slip marker (sl m), p4, sl m, k4, [p4, k4] 3 times, sl m, p4, sl m, [k4, p4] 2 times, k1, p1, k1.

ROWS 3–8: Rep Rows 1 and 2 two more times.

ROW 9: K1, p1, k1, [yo] 2 times, *work the sts as they appear to m, sl m, M1R, k2, M1L, sl m; rep from * once, work the sts as they appear to last 3 sts, [yo] 2 times, k1, p1, k1—82 sts.

ROW 10: K1, p1, k2tog (next st and first wrap of double yo), p1 (second wrap of double yo), work the sts as they appear to next double yo, p1 (first wrap of double yo), k2tog (second wrap of double yo and next st), p1, k1—80 sts.

ROW 11: K1, p1, k1, M1R, *work the sts as they appear to m, sl m, M1R, k4, M1L, sl m; rep from * once, work the sts as they appear to last 3 sts, M1L, k1, p1, k1—86 sts.

ROWS 12, 14, AND 16: K1, p1, k1, work the sts as they appear to last 3 sts, k1, p1, k1.

ROWS 13 AND 15: Rep Row 11—98 sts after Row 15.

Note: When the sections between markers are increased to 12 sts, move the markers to just before and just after the center 4 sts.

ROWS 17–66: Rep Rows 9–16 six more times, then work Rows 9 and 10 once more—248 sts after Row 66.

ROWS 67–72: Rep Rows 11 and 12 three times—266 sts.

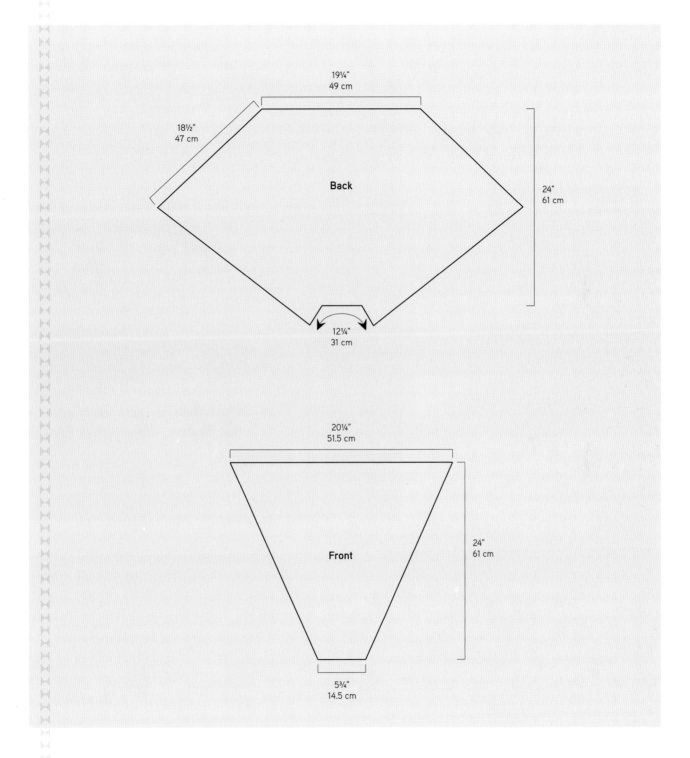

19¼"
49 cm

18½"
47 cm

Back

24"
61 cm

12¼"
31 cm

20¼"
51.5 cm

Front

24"
61 cm

5¾"
14.5 cm

Work even for 1½" (3.8 cm). Rep Rows 11 and 12 four times—290 sts. Work even for 2" (5 cm). Rep Rows 11 and 12 four times—314 sts. Work even for 3" (7.5 cm). Rep Rows 11 and 12 four times—338 sts. Work even until piece measures 23¼" (59 cm) from CO.

NEXT ROW: *K1, p1; rep from * to last st, k1.

Rep the last row 3 more times. Loosely BO all sts in patt.

Finishing

Wet-block pieces and pin to finished measurements. Let air-dry completely before removing pins.

Cut Ultrasuede tape into two pieces, each 2 yd (1.8 m) long. Lace the Ultrasuede through the two pieces like lacing a shoe as foll: With RS facing, place front next to back so that edges touch along one side. Beg at top, thread one strip of Ultrasuede up through first double yo of both pieces, *bring the right-hand end over to left and down through next hole; bring left-hand end over to right and down through next hole, bring right-hand end up through next hole on left, bring left-hand end up through next hole on right; rep from * 2 more times, then thread Ultrasuede down through rem holes. Rep on other side.

Instead of Ultrasuede ribbon, you could knit I-cord for the laces. For a completely different look, add beautiful buttons opposite the buttonholes and along the diagonal lines of the raglan increases and omit the laces altogether.

sand dollar
BELTED LACE CAPE

Inspired by the geometric pattern of sand dollars along the beach, I set out to create an overlapped fabric that incorporated slits for armholes or belt loops. The result is this cape, which is shaped as a large circle with a front opening. The yoke is a beautiful, easy-to-memorize flower petal lace pattern that is worked from the neck down. To form the slits, the yoke is divided into strips that are knitted individually, then overlapped and joined in a garter-stitch band at the bottom. A simple picot bind-off adds a delicate look to the hem. Wear this piece as a traditional cape or use the slits as armholes or belt loops to create wide flowing sleeves.

NOTES

- When blocking the cape into a large flat circle, utilize the picot hem for accurate pinning.

- To make working this pattern easier, place markers after each repeat on the first row, then slip markers every row as you come to them.

- See the accompanying DVD for a demonstration on working the overlapped panels and picot bind-off.

MATERIALS

FINISHED SIZE
About 50" (127 cm) in diameter and 22" (56 cm) long.

YARN
DK weight (#3 Light).

shown here: Green Mountain Spinnery Cotton Comfort (20% organic cotton, 80% fine wool; 180 yd [164 m]/2 oz): #6714 Maize, 10 skeins.

NEEDLES
Size U.S. 7 (4.5 mm): 16" and 32" (40 and 80 cm) circular (cir). *Adjust needle size if necessary to obtain the correct gauge.*

NOTIONS
Markers (m); stitch holders; tapestry needle.

GAUGE
21 stitches and 20 rows = 4" (10 cm) in lace pattern, blocked.

When the waist is cinched with a wide belt, this wrap looks very much like a cardigan with wide, billowing sleeves . . . and gives a slimming illusion. ◄►◄►

Cape

With longer cir needle, CO 52 sts. Work Rows 1–44 of Sand Dollar A chart—724 sts. Work Rows 1–4 of Sand Dollar B chart—770 sts.

Note: Each of the 12 sections is worked separately on the shorter cir needle for Sand Dollar C chart, then placed on st holders when completed.

*Work Rows 1–14 of Sand Dollar C chart—56 sts rem. Rep Rows 13 and 14 of Sand Dollar C chart twenty more times—section measures about 10¾" (27.5 cm) from division. Cut yarn and place sts on holder.

NEXT PANEL: With shorter cir needle, CO 2 sts and sl next 64 sts onto the same needle—56 sts total. Rep from * for rem 11 panels—12 panels total.

Finishing

Note: Each of the 12 panels will be joined together on the next row, but overlapped, knitting one-third of each section simultaneously with the adjacent panel: The 2nd, 3rd, 4th, 5th, and 6th panels are joined behind the 1st, 2nd, 3rd, 4th, and 5th panels, respectively, then the 7th panel is knitted next to the 6th panel (without overlapping), then the 8th, 9th, 10th, 11th, and 12 panels are joined in front of the 7th, 8th, 9th, 10th, and 11th panels, respectively.

Join Panels

With longer cir needle and RS facing, k38 sts of 1st panel, hold 2nd panel behind 1st panel, knit the last 18 sts of 1st panel tog with first 18 sts of 2nd panel, k20 in center of 2nd panel, hold 3rd panel behind 2nd panel, knit the last 18 sts of 2nd panel tog with the first 18 sts of 3rd panel, k20 in center of 3rd panel, hold 4th panel behind 3rd panel, knit the last 18 sts of 3rd panel tog with first 18 sts of 4th panel, k20 sts in center of 4th panel, hold 5th panel behind 4th panel, knit the last 18 sts of 4th panel tog with first 18 sts of 5th panel, k20 sts in center of 5th panel, hold 6th panel behind 5th panel, knit the last 18 sts of 5th panel tog with first 18 sts of 6th panel, k38 rem sts of 6th panel. Do not cut yarn. Join the left side as foll: k38 sts of 7th panel, hold 8th panel in front of 7th panel, knit the last 18 sts of the 7th panel tog with the first 18 sts on the 8th panel, k20 sts in center of 8th panel, hold 9th panel in front of 8th panel, knit the last 18 sts of 8th panel tog with first 18 sts of 9th panel, k20 sts in center of 9th panel, hold

Sand Dollar Chart A

work 12 times

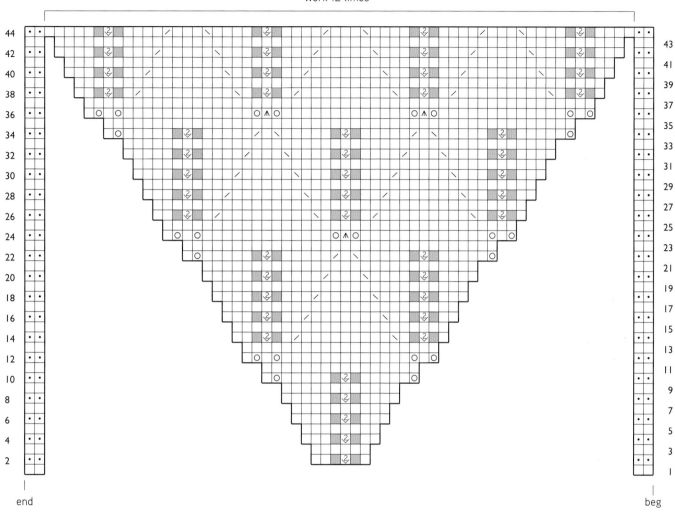

k on RS; p on WS

· p on RS; k on WS

○ yo

╱ k2tog

╲ ssk

no stitch

(k1, yo, k1) in same st

∧ sl 1, k2tog, psso

pattern repeat

Sand Dollar Chart B

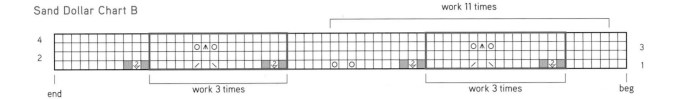

work 11 times

end · work 3 times · work 3 times · beg

Sand Dollar Chart C

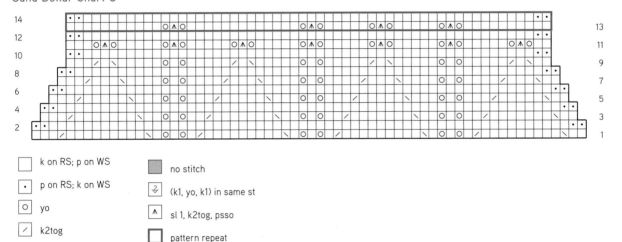

	k on RS; p on WS		no stitch
·	p on RS; k on WS	⍖	(k1, yo, k1) in same st
O	yo	⋀	sl 1, k2tog, psso
╱	k2tog		pattern repeat
╲	ssk		

10th panel in front of 9th panel, knit the last 18 sts of the 9th panel tog with the first 18 sts of the 10th panel, k20 sts in center of 10th panel, hold 11th panel in front of 10th panel, knit last 18 sts of 10th panel tog with first 18 sts of 11th panel, k20 sts in center of 11th panel, hold 12th panel held in front of 11th panel, knit last 18 sts of 11th panel tog with first 18 sts of 12th panel, k38 rem sts of 12th panel—492 sts total.

Knit every row for 15 more rows—piece measures about 1½" (3.8 cm) from joining row. Use a variation of the picot method (see page 23) to BO all sts as foll: BO 3 sts, *sl rem st on right needle tip to left needle tip, use knitted method (see Glossary) to CO 3 sts, BO 10 (the 3 sts just

CO plus the st used to beg the knitted CO, plus the next 6 sts); rep from * to last 3 sts, sl rem st from right needle tip onto left needle tip, use the knitted method to CO 3 sts, BO to end.

Weave in loose ends. Wet-block and pin to finished measurements. Let air-dry completely before removing pins.

infinity
CARDI-WRAP WITH SLEEVES

This cardi-wrap begins with a large infinity motif that forms the sweater back. I used a self-striping yarn to emphasize the multiple directions of rows that make up the motif. The sides are picked up along the edges of the back and are worked in a light and airy openwork pattern that resembles crocheted broomstick lace. For no-sew construction, the collar and sleeves are picked up and worked outward from the body. Wear this wrap hanging open or pinned at the front or make long I-cord ties attached to each side of the front at your natural waist, then wrap the ties around the fronts, loop them through the openwork, around the back, and, finally, tie them in the front.

NOTES

- See the accompanying DVD for a demonstration on working the short-row shaping and 3/3 crossed-loop stitches.

MATERIALS

FINISHED SIZE
About 42½" (108 cm) wide and 32" (81.5 cm) long, excluding collar.

YARN
Chunky weight (#5 Bulky).

shown here: Tahki Presto (48% wool, 46% acrylic, 3% mohair, 3% nylon; 60 yd [55 m]/50 g): #002 Curry, 15 balls.

NEEDLES
Size U.S. 10 (6 mm): 32" (60 cm) circular (cir). *Adjust needle size if necessary to obtain the correct gauge.*

NOTIONS
Contrasting waste yarn for stitch holders; tapestry needle.

GAUGE
14 stitches and 20 rows = 4" (10 cm) in stockinette stitch with garter ridges; 13 stitches and 17 rows = 4" (10 cm) in garter and twisted drop stitch.

Back

CO 1 st, place marker (pm), CO 20 sts, [pm, CO 24 sts] 6 times—165 sts total. Do not join.

ROW 1: [K1, k2tog, k21] 6 times, k20, ([k1, p1] 3 times) in the same st—164 sts.

ROW 2: Purl.

ROW 3: [K11, k2tog, k10] 6 times, k20, [k1f&b (see Glossary)] 6 times.

ROW 4: Knit.

ROW 5: [K20, k2tog] 6 times, k20, [k1, k1f&b] 6 times.

ROW 6: Purl.

ROW 7: [K10, k2tog, k9] 6 times, k20, [k2, k1f&b] 6 times.

ROW 8: Knit.

ROW 9: [K18, k2tog] 6 times, k20, [k1f&b, k3] 6 times.

ROW 10: Purl.

ROW 11: [K9, k2tog, k8] 6 times, k20, [k2, k1f&b, k2] 6 times.

ROW 12: Knit.

ROW 13: [K16, k2tog] 6 times, k20, [k5, k1f&b] 6 times.

ROW 14: Purl.

ROW 15: [K15, k2tog] 6 times, k20, [k1f&b, k6] 6 times.

ROW 16: Knit.

ROW 17: [K8, k2tog, k6] 6 times, k20, [k3, k1f&b, k4] 6 times.

ROW 18: Purl.

ROW 19: [K1, k2tog, k12] 6 times, k20, [k1, k1f&b, k7] 6 times.

ROW 20: Knit.

ROW 21: [K5, k2tog, k7] 6 times, k20, [k5, k1f&b, k4] 6 times.

ROW 22: Purl.

3/3 Crossed Loops

For this stitch, I chose to encase the first, second, and third loops inside the fourth, fifth, and sixth to create an unusual texture. A more traditional approach would be to just cross one set in front of the other. Try it both ways to see which you prefer.

Sl 6 sts purlwise onto right needle tip while dropping extra yo wraps (**Figure 1**). Counting the sts from left to right, insert left needle tip into the 4th, 5th, and 6th sts to encase the first 3 sts (**Figure 2**), return the rem 3 sts onto the left needle tip (**Figure 3**), then knit these 6 sts in the new order.

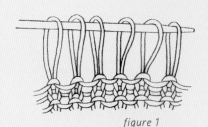

figure 1

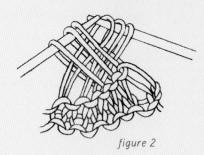

figure 2

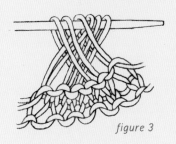

figure 3

Assembly Diagram

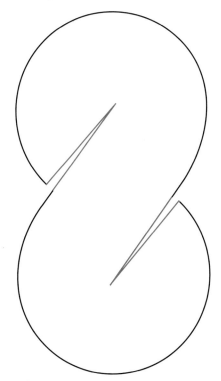

Sew side edges to cast-on and
bind-off edges along red lines.

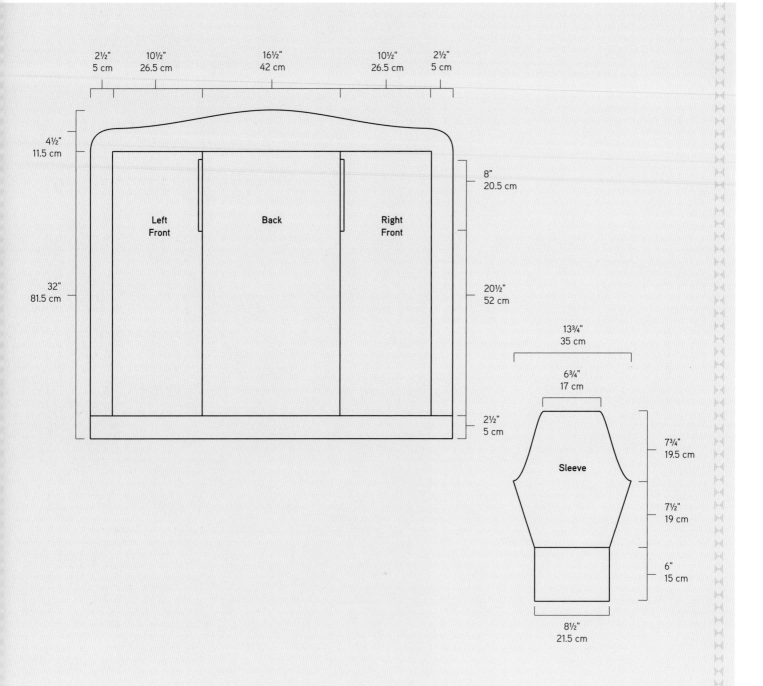

2½"
5 cm

10½"
26.5 cm

16½"
42 cm

10½"
26.5 cm

2½"
5 cm

4½"
11.5 cm

8"
20.5 cm

Left
Front

Back

Right
Front

32"
81.5 cm

20½"
52 cm

13¾"
35 cm

6¾"
17 cm

2½"
5 cm

7¾"
19.5 cm

Sleeve

7½"
19 cm

6"
15 cm

8½"
21.5 cm

ROW 23: [K7, k2tog, k4] 6 times, k20, [K7, k1f&b, k3] 6 times.

ROW 24: Knit.

ROW 25: [K9, k2tog, k1] 6 times, k20, [k9, k1f&b, k2] 6 times.

ROW 26: Purl.

ROW 27: [K1, k2tog, k8] 6 times, k20, [k11, k1f&b, k1] 6 times.

ROW 28: Knit.

ROW 29: [K3, k2tog, k5] 6 times, k20, [k13, k1f&b] 6 times.

ROW 30: Purl.

ROW 31: [K5, k2tog, k2] 6 times, k20, [k1, k1f&b, k13] 6 times.

ROW 32: Knit.

ROW 33: [K6, k2tog] 6 times, k20, [k3, k1f&b, k12] 6 times.

ROW 34: Purl.

ROW 35: [K1, k2tog, k4] 6 times, k20, [k5, k1f&b, k11] 6 times.

ROW 36: Knit.

ROW 37: [K2, k2tog, k2] 6 times, k20, [k7, k1f&b, k11] 6 times.

ROW 38: Purl.

ROW 39: [K3, k2tog] 6 times, k20, [k9, k1f&b, k9] 6 times.

ROW 40: Knit.

ROW 41: [K2, k2tog] 6 times, [k11, k1f&b, k8] 6 times.

ROW 42: Purl.

ROW 43: [K2tog, k1] 6 times, k20, [k13, k1f&b, k7] 6 times.

ROW 44: Knit.

ROW 45: [K2tog] 6 times, k20, [k1, k1f&b, k20] 6 times.

ROW 46: Purl.

A deceptively easy lace stitch complements the bulky yarn for a light, drapey look and feel for the fronts and sleeves of this wrap.

ROW 47: Sl 4 purlwise with yarn in back, k3tog, p4sso, k20, [k4, k1f&b, k18] 6 times.

BO all sts. Block. With yarn threaded on a tapestry needle and foll the Assembly Diagram on page 51, sew CO and BO edges to selvedge edges of center section as shown.

Right Front

ROW 1: With RS facing and beg 48 sts below the center seam, pick up and knit 48 sts long right-hand side of back to center seam, pick up and knit 20 more sts, then use the knitted method (see Glossary) to CO 24 sts, skip the next 24 sts of the back for the armhole, then pick up and knit the next 4 sts—96 sts total.

ROWS 2–6: Knit.

ROW 7: *[Yo] 2 times, k1; rep from *—288 sts.

ROW 8: *Work 3/3 crossed loops (see page 50); rep from *—96 sts rem.

ROWS 9–14: Knit.

ROWS 15 AND 16: Rep Rows 7 and 8.

Rep Rows 9–16 three more times, then rep Rows 9–14 once more—piece measures about 10½" (26.5 cm) from pick-up row.

Place sts on contrasting waste yarn holder that is twice as long as the width of the rem sts.

Left Front

ROW 1: With RS facing and beg 48 sts above the center seam, pick up and knit 4 sts along side of back, use the knitted method to CO 24 sts, skip the next 24 sts of the back for the armhole, then pick up and knit 68 sts—96 sts total. Work as for right front.

Collar and Front Bands

With RS facing and beg 12 sts to the right of the center back, work as foll:

ROW 1: *Pick up and knit 3 sts, pick up and purl (see Glossary) 3 sts; rep from * 3 more times—24 sts.

ROW 2: *K3, p3; rep from * to end of row, then pick up and knit 3 more sts—27 sts.

ROW 3: *P3, k3; rep from * 3 more times, p3, then pick up and knit 3 more sts—30 sts.

ROW 4: *P3, k3; rep from * 4 more times, then pick up and purl 3 more sts—33 sts.

ROW 5: *K3, p3; rep from * 4 more times, k3, then pick up and purl 3 more sts—36 sts.

ROW 6: *K3, p3 rep from * 5 more times, then pick up and knit 3 more sts—39 sts.

ROW 7: *P3, k3; rep from * 5 more times, p3, then pick up and knit 3 more sts—42 sts.

ROW 8: *P3, k3; rep from * 6 more times, then pick up and purl 3 more sts in edge of garter rows along edge of front—45 sts.

ROW 9: *K3, p3; rep from * 6 more times, k3, then pick up and purl 3 more sts in edge of garter rows along edge of front—48 sts.

ROW 10: *K3, p3; rep from * 7 more times, then (pick up and knit 1 st, yo, pick up and knit 1 more st) in space from edge of twisted drop-stitch row—51 sts.

ROW 11: *P3, k3; rep from * 7 more times, p3, then (pick up and knit 1 st, yo, pick up and k1 more st) in space from edge of twisted drop-stitch row—54 sts.

ROW 12: *P3, k3; rep from * 8 more times, then pick up and purl 3 more sts in edge of garter rows along edge of front—57 sts.

ROW 13: *K3, p3; rep from * 8 more times, k3, then pick up and purl 3 more sts in edge of garter rows along edge of front—60 sts.

ROW 14: Working in patt as established, pick up and knit 24 sts along top edge, stopping 3 rows before corners, pick up and knit 1 st in each of the next 3 rows, work 96 held front sts as foll: k1f&b, (k1, p1) in next st, p1f&b, *k3, p3; rep from *—186 sts.

ROW 15: Rep Row 14—312 sts.

ROWS 16–22: Work in patt as established.

Maintaining k3, p3 rib patt, use a modification of the yarnover method (see page 106) to loosely BO as foll: P1, *[yo, p1, use the left needle tip to pick up the first st and yo and pass them both off the needle—1 st rem on right needle tip] 3 times, [yo, k1, use the left needle tip to pick up the first st and yo and pass them both off the needle—1 st rem on right needle tip] 3 times; rep from * until 1 st rem. Fasten off last st.

Sleeves

Note: The sleeve cap is picked up from the top center of the sleeve opening, with additional sts picked up at the end of every row until the entire sleeve opening is picked up and on the needles.

In general, pick up one-third of the number of sts for sleeve opening across the top, centering them over the shoulder seam, then pick up 1 additional st at the end of every row until you have picked up every st around the armhole.

ROW 1: With RS facing and beg 12 sts before shoulder seam, pick up and knit 24 sts.

ROWS 2, 4, 6, 8, 10, 12, 14, AND 16: (WS) Purl to end, pick up and purl 1 st—1 st inc'd each row; 39 sts after Row 16.

ROWS 3, 5, 7, 9, 11, 13, 15, AND 17: (RS) Knit to end, pick up and knit 1 st—1 st inc'd each row; 40 sts after Row 17.

ROWS 18 AND 20: Knit to end, pick up and knit 2 sts—2 sts inc'd each row; 46 sts after Row 20.

ROWS 19 AND 21: Purl to end, pick up and purl 2 sts—2 sts inc'd each row; 48 sts after Row 21.

Place marker (pm) and join for working in rnds. Work even in St st (knit every rnd) until piece measures 4" (10 cm) from joining rnd.

DEC RND: K2tog, knit to last 2 sts, ssk—2 sts dec'd.

Knit 3 rnds even.

Rep the last 4 rnds 8 more times—30 sts rem.

Cuff

RNDS 1, 3, 5, AND 7: Knit.

RNDS 2, 4, 6, AND 8: Purl.

RND 9: *[Yo] 2 times, k1; rep from *—90 sts.

RND 10: *Sl 6 sts onto right needle tip while dropping extra yo's, insert left needle tip into the front of the 1st, 2nd, and 3rd of these sts and pass them over the 4th, 5th, and 6th sts to encase the first 3 sts, return these 6 to the left needle tip in their new order, then knit these 6 sts; rep from *—30 sts.

Rep Rnds 1–10 once, then rep Rnds 1–8 once more. Loosely BO all sts.

Finishing
Bottom Edging

ROW 1: With RS facing and beg at lower edge of left front, pick up and knit 3 sts, pick up and purl 3 sts along edge of front band, *pick up and knit 3 sts in end of garter rows of left front, pick up and (p1, yo, p1) in space in edge of twisted drop-st row; rep from * 4 more times, pick up and knit 3 sts in end of garter rows, [pick up and purl 3 sts, pick up and knit 3 sts] 6 times along lower edge of back, **pick up and purl 3 sts in end of garter rows of right front, pick up and (k1, yo, k1) in space in edge of twisted drop-st row; rep from ** 4 more times, pick up and purl 3 sts in end of garter rows, then pick up and knit 3 sts and pick up and purl 3 sts along edge of right front band—114 sts total.

ROWS 2–12: *K3, p3; rep from *.

Maintaining k3, p3 rib patt, use a modification of the yarnover method to loosely BO as foll: K1, *[yo, k1, use the left needle tip to pick up the first st and yo and pass them both off the needle—1 st rem on right needle tip] 3 times, [yo, p1, use the left needle tip to pick up the first st and yo and pass them both off the needle—1 st rem on right needle tip] 3 times; rep from * until 1 st rem. Fasten off last st.

Weave in loose ends. Wet-block and pin to finished measurements. Let air-dry completely before removing pins.

tree of life
EMBROIDERED RUANA

This ruana pays fiber homage to Tim Parish's painting *Tree of Life;* I learned to knit intarsia specifically to create the contrasting trunk. The free-form swirling tree branches are added with chain-stitch embroidery after the piece is knitted. The body of this ruana is knitted in a reversible non-curling texture stitch, but the tree trunk is knitted in stockinette stitch to blend with the embroidery and to contrast against the textured background. Box pleats in the yoke and a self-tie belt provide shaping and design details on the front. The yarn, a merino roving wool that is airy and soft, provides plenty of texture for hiding the loose ends woven in the wrong side.

NOTES

- See the accompanying DVD for a demonstration on working the pleats.

MATERIALS

FINISHED SIZE
About 25" (63.5 cm) wide at back and 22½" (57 cm) long.

YARN
Worsted weight (#4 Medium).

shown here: Stacey Charles Collezione Tinka (100% merino; 108 yd [100 m]/50 g): #02 Coffee (MC), 8 balls; #04 Dark Olive (CC), 1 ball.

NEEDLES
Size U.S. 8 (5 mm): 32" (80 cm) circular (cir) and set of double-pointed (dpn) for box pleat. *Adjust needle size if necessary to obtain the correct gauge.*

NOTIONS
Stitch holders; tapestry needle.

GAUGE
17 stitches and 19 rows = 4" (10 cm) in moss stitch.

Right Front

With MC, CO 64 sts.

ROWS 1 AND 2: K1, p1; rep from *.

ROWS 3 AND 4: P1, k1; rep from *.

Rep Rows 1–4 until piece measures 21"
(53.5 cm) from CO, ending with a WS row.

PLEAT ROW: (RS) Work 20 sts, work 24-st box
pleat (see box at right), work to end—48 sts
rem. Rep Rows 1–4 for 6" (15 cm) more. Place
sts on holder.

Left Front

With MC, CO and work as right front.

24-Stitch Box Pleat

Switching to double-pointed needles for the box pleat gives you ample
room to fold the fabric in the appropriate direction before joining the
pleats. Practice the fold before knitting through all layers of fabric to
help understand how the completed pleat will look.

First half of pleat: Sl 4 sts onto dpn for underlay, sl next 4 sts onto
dpn for fold-under, hold fold-under behind left-hand needle with WS
tog, then hold underlay behind fold-under with RS tog—3 needles held
tog on the left. *Insert right-hand needle into first st on all 3 left-hand
needles and work these sts tog (3 sts made into 1); rep from *—4 pleat
sts on right needle.

Second half of pleat: Sl 4 sts onto dpn for top, sl next 4 sts onto dpn
for fold-under, hold fold-under in front of left-hand needle with RS tog,
then hold top over fold-under with WS tog—3 needles held tog at left of
work. *Insert right-hand needle into first st on all 3 left-hand needles
and work these sts tog (3 sts made into 1); rep from *—8 sts rem.

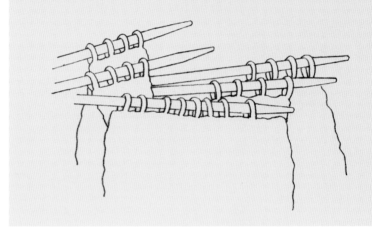

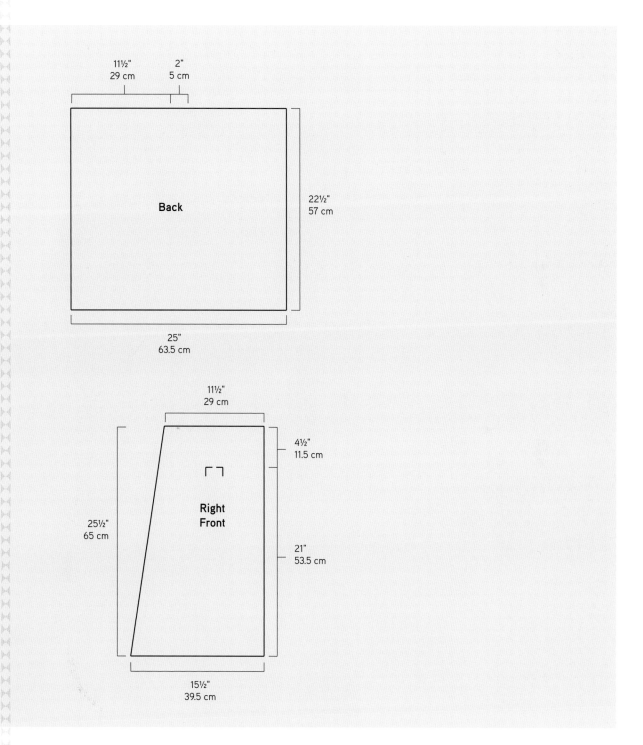

11½"
29 cm

2"
5 cm

Back

22½"
57 cm

25"
63.5 cm

11½"
29 cm

4½"
11.5 cm

**Right
Front**

25½"
65 cm

21"
53.5 cm

15½"
39.5 cm

Back

With MC, CO 100 sts.

ROWS 1 AND 2: K1, p1; rep from *.

ROWS 3 AND 4: P1, k1; rep from *.

Rep Rows 1–4 until piece measure 4¼" (11 cm) from CO. Working MC sts in patt as established and CC sts in St st (knit RS rows; purl WS rows), work center 33 sts according to Rows 1–52 of Colorwork chart.

With MC, cont in rib as foll: rep Rows 1–4 seven times, then rep Rows 1 and 2 once more—piece measures about 22½" (57 cm) from CO.

With RS facing tog, use the three-needle method (see Glossary) to BO the first 48 sts of back to 48 right front sts, then BO 2 center back sts as normal, then use the three-needle method to BO rem 48 sts of back to 48 left front sts. Fasten off.

Use the chart and illustration to adapt this pattern into a pillow, tote bag, or blanket, adjusting the number of stitches as necessary to the desired width and centering the chart.

Colorwork Chart

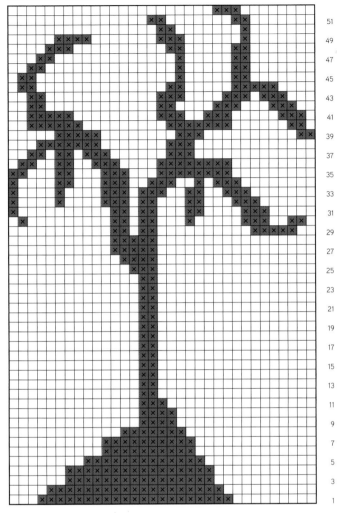

51
49
47
45
43
41
39
37
35
33
31
29
27
25
23
21
19
17
15
13
11
9
7
5
3
1

☐ coffee (MC), worked in moss st

☒ dark olive (CC), k on RS; p on WS

Finishing

Weave in loose ends. Wet-block and pin to finished measurements. Let air-dry completely before removing pins.

With CC threaded on a tapestry needle, work chain-stitch embroidery (see Glossary) to add free-form branches to tree motif as shown in Embroidery Diagram on page 64.

Belt

With RS facing and beg 8" (20.5 cm) up from lower edge, pick up and knit 10 sts along edge of back. Work in k1, p1 rib until piece measures 18" (45.5 cm) from pick-up row.

Rep on other side of back.

ring of cables
OVAL SHRUG

Shrugs have remained popular over the decades because they flatter the figure and complement many outfits. In this design, I pay homage to a variety of cables for unusual texture in a thick, warm wrap. The body is worked back and forth in rows in a pretty cable and rib pattern. Through two series of short-rows, the flat fabric is manipulated into a long oval shape. The collar is picked up from the body and worked in a cable pattern against a k1, p1 ribbed foundation to form reversible fabric. Wear the collar standing up for drama or fold it over for a more casual look.

MATERIALS

FINISHED SIZE
About 24 (27½)" (61 [70] cm) wide and 13" (33 cm) long.

YARN
Worsted weight (#4 Medium).

shown here: Malabrigo Worsted (100% merino; 210 yd [192 m]/ 100 g): #52 Paris Nights, 3 (3) skeins.

NEEDLES
Size U.S. 8 (5 mm): 24" (60 cm) circular (cir). Ribbing: size U.S. 9 (5.5 mm): 32" (80 cm) cir. *Adjust needle size if necessary to obtain the correct gauge.*

NOTIONS
Contrasting waste yarn for provision-al cast-on; cable needle (cn); markers (m); tapestry needle.

GAUGE
24 stitches and 24 rows = 4" (10 cm) in cable pattern with smaller needle; 25 stitches = 4" (10 cm) in ribbing pattern with larger needle.

2/2 LC

Sl 2 sts onto cn and hold in front, k2, k2 from cn.

2/2 RC

Sl 2 sts onto cn and hold in back, k2, k2 from cn.

8/8 LC in Ribbing

Sl 8 sts onto cn and hold in front, [k1, p1] 4 times, [k1, p1] 4 times from cn.

8/8 RC in Ribbing

Sl 8 sts onto cn and hold in back, [k1, p1] 4 times, [k1, p1] 4 times from cn.

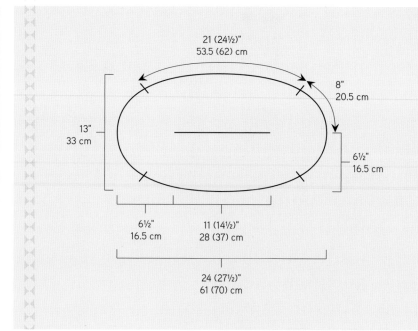

Back Cable

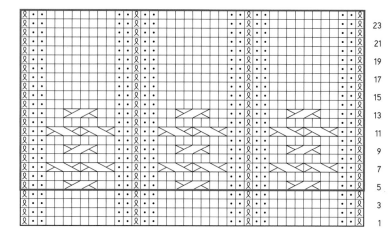

Edging and Collar Cable

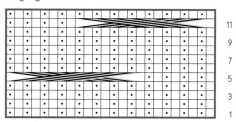

	k on RS; p on WS
•	p on RS; k on WS
ℓ	k1 tbl on RS; p1 tbl on WS
c	short-row wrap and turn (see Glossary)
	2/2 RC (see box at top right)
	2/2 LC (see box at top right)
	8/8 LC in Ribbing (see box at top left)
	8/8 RC in Ribbing (see box at top left)
	pattern repeat

Back

With waste yarn and working yarn, use a provisional method (see Glossary) to CO 40 sts.

Work Rows 1–24 of Back Cable chart, then rep Rows 5–24 one (two) more times, then work Rows 5–14 once more—54 (74) rows total. Work Rows 1–160 of Short-Row chart (see pages 70 and 71), hiding wraps by working them tog with wrapped sts when you come to them on subsequent rows (see Glossary).

Rep Rows 1 and 2 of Back Cable chart, then rep Rows 5–24 of Back Cable chart three (four) more times, then rep Rows 5–14 once more, then rep Rows 1–160 of Short-Row chart, then rep Rows 1 and 2 of Back Cable chart, then rep Rows 5–20 of Back Cable chart once more—piece measures about 11½ (15)" (29 [38] cm) from CO along edge at center of oval between sets of short-rows.

Finishing

Carefully remove the waste yarn from the provisional CO and place the live sts on a needle. Use the three-needle BO method (see Glossary) to join the exposed CO sts to the last row of knitting to form a ring. With yarn threaded on a tapestry needle and RS facing, use the mattress st (see Glossary) to sew up the center of the ring to form an oval (oval shape will become more obvious after blocking). Wet-block and pin to finished measurements. Let air-dry completely before removing pins.

◁▷◁▷ *Don't be concerned if the shrug doesn't look like an oval before blocking. The ribbing and cables condense the fabric, and proper pinning and blocking are needed to achieve the oval shape. Blocking will help you see where to pick up stitches for the collar, too.*

Edging and Collar

With WS tog, fold oval in half along center seam. Mark both edges on each side of oval about 8" (20.5 cm) from fold for armhole placement.

With RS facing and using larger cir needle, pick up and knit 120 (130) sts along one long side of the oval, turn and pick up 120 (130) sts along the other long side of the oval—240 (260) sts total. Place marker (pm) and join for working in rnds.

Note: Omitting the shorter sides of the oval when joining in the round creates the beginning of the sleeves.

SET-UP RND: *[K1, p1] 2 times, (k1, p1) in same st; rep from *—288 (312) sts.

Rep Rnds 1–12 of Edging and Collar Cable chart until edging measures about 6" (15 cm) from pick-up rnd, ending with Rnd 5 or 11. Use a modification of the yarnover method (see page 106) to BO loosely in rib as foll: K1, *yo, p1, insert left needle tip into the first knit st and yo, and pass both off the needle, leaving purl st on right needle tip, yo, k1, insert left needle tip into first purl st and yo and pass both off the needle, leaving knit right needle tip; rep from *.

With yarn threaded on a tapestry needle, sew 2½ (2)" (6.5 [5] cm) sleeve seams from the beginning of the edging to the sleeve edge. Weave in loose ends. Block again.

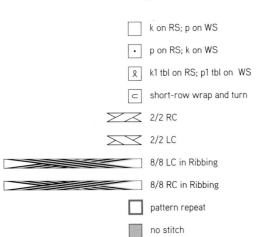

☐	k on RS; p on WS
•	p on RS; k on WS
ℛ	k1 tbl on RS; p1 tbl on WS
⊂	short-row wrap and turn
⧄	2/2 RC
⧅	2/2 LC
	8/8 LC in Ribbing
	8/8 RC in Ribbing
☐	pattern repeat
▓	no stitch

Short Row 1–81

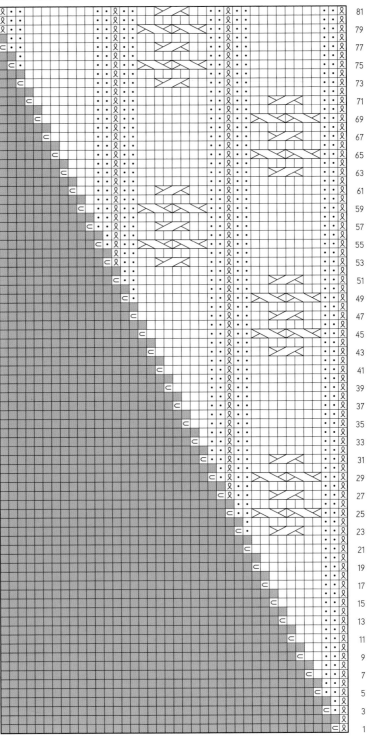

Short Row 82–160

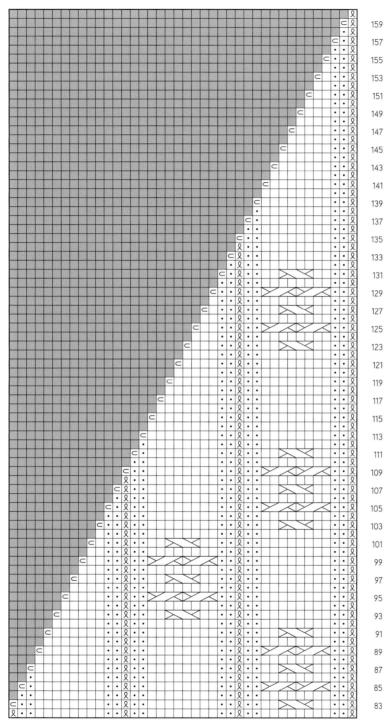

159
157
155
153
151
149
147
145
143
141
139
137
135
133
131
129
127
125
123
121
119
117
115
113
111
109
107
105
103
101
99
97
95
93
91
89
87
85
83

summit
AMERICAN YAK WRAP

I designed this wrap as an experiment in joining knitted lace strips to create a reversible rectangular wrap with arm openings. The two center strips are worked in three separate pieces to accommodate the armholes; the outside strips extend the full width of the wrap. The strips are joined in a method similar to a three-needle bind-off, but worked over two rows—the stitches are knitted together on the first row, then bound off on the second row. The wrap is finished with two types of edging—the first is worked in the round to form a border around the joined strips, the second is worked perpendicularly to the live stitches.

NOTES

- A monochromatic wrap will require 6 skeins total.

- This lace-stitch pattern is reversible, not because the stitches are identical on both sides, but because there is an odd number of rows in the repeat—every other repeat has an opposite right side. Theoretically, you could add an additional row to any stitch pattern to make it reversible in this fashion.

- See the accompanying DVD for a demonstration on joining the strip motifs and working the bobbles.

MATERIALS

FINISHED SIZE
About 22" (56 cm) wide and 58¼" (148 cm) long. Each small strip measures 3½" (9 cm) wide and 16¾" (42.5 cm) long; each large strip measures 3½" (9 cm) wide and 50¼" (127 cm) long.

YARN
Sportweight (#2 Fine).

shown here: Bijou Basin Ranch 50/50 Yak/Cormo Wool Blend (50% yak, 50% American Cormo; 150 yd [137 m]/2 oz): Cream (A), 5 skeins; Heathered Gray Brown (B) 1 skein.

NEEDLES
Size U.S. 7 (4.5 mm): straight, 32" (80 cm) circular (cir), and one double-pointed (dpn). *Adjust needle size if necessary to obtain the correct gauge.*

NOTIONS
Markers (m); tapestry needle.

GAUGE
10½ stitches and 20 rows = 4" (10 cm) in lace pattern, after blocking.

Bobble (MB)

([K1, p1] 2 times, k1) in same st to make 5 sts, turn work, [k5, turn work] 3 times, k5tog—1 st.

Short Strip (make 6)

With A and straight needles, CO 44 sts.

ROW 1: K1, *yo, k1; rep from * to last st, k1—86 sts.

ROW 2: K1, purl to last st, k1.

ROW 3: K1, *k2tog; rep from * to last st, k1—44 sts rem.

ROWS 4 AND 5: K1, *yo, k2tog; rep from * to last st, k1.

ROWS 6 AND 7: Knit.

Rep Rows 1–7 once, then rep Rows 1–3 once more—piece measures about 3½" (9 cm) from CO. Use the yarnover method (see page 106) to BO as foll: K1, *yo k1, insert left needle tip into both yo and first st on right needle tip, and lift them over the last st on right needle; rep from *. Fasten off last st.

Long Strip (make 2)

With A and straight needles, CO 132 sts.

ROW 1: K1, *yo, k1; rep from * to last st, k1—262 sts.

ROW 2: K1, purl to last st, k1.

ROW 3: K1, *K2tog; rep from * to last st, k1—132 sts rem.

ROWS 4 AND 5: K1, *yo, k2 tog; rep from * to last st, k1.

ROWS 6 AND 7: Knit.

Rep Rows 1–7 once, then rep Rows 1–3 once more—piece measures about 3½" (9 cm) from CO. BO as for short strip.

Join Strips

Notes: For an element of color and design, join strips with B; for a more uniform look, join strips with A.

Holding 2 strips tog, pick up and knit through the large holes formed by yarnovers in the BO row of both thicknesses for the same number of stitches as were CO as foll.

Joining Two Short Strips (make 3 sets of 2 joined short strips)

ROW 1: Holding both strips together, pick up and knit 44 sts along CO edge.

ROW 2: Use the yarnover method to BO as foll: K1, *yo, k1, use left needle tip to pick both the first knit st and yo over the other knit st and off the needles (1 st rem on right needle tip); rep from *—1 st rem.

Fasten off.

Joining Diagram

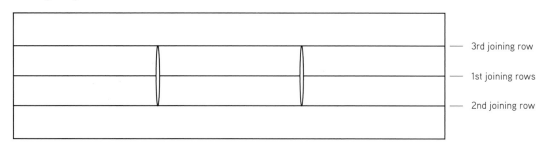

— 3rd joining row

— 1st joining rows

— 2nd joining row

Joining Short-Strip Pairs to Long Strips

Following the schematic on page 74, work as foll:

ROW 1: Holding the edge of one short strip tog with the beg of a long strip, pick up and knit 44 sts, hold second short strip together with middle of same long strip with end next to end of first short strip, pick up and knit 44 sts, hold third short strip together with end of same long strip with end next to end of second short strip, pick up and knit 44 sts—132 sts total.

ROW 2: Use the yarnover method to BO as before.

Fasten off.

Repeat Rows 1 and 2 to join the opposite side of the short strips to the second long strip.

Finishing

First Edging

Note: This edging is worked in garter stitch (alternate knit 1 rnd, purl 1 rnd); place a marker (m) before each corner st to remind you to work corner incs.

RND 1: With B, cir needle, RS facing, and beg at one corner, pick up and knit 12 sts along the short edge of each strip, 1 st in each join, 1 st in each corner, and 132 sts along the long side of each strip—370 sts total.

Place marker (pm) and join for working in rnds.

◀ ▶ ◀ ▶ *For a solid rectangular wrap without sleeve openings, knit five long strips and join them accordingly. Knit and join only three long strips for a beautiful scarf.*

RND 2: Purl.

RND 3: With A, k1, M1 (see Glossary), *knit to 2 sts before corner m, M1, k1, slip marker (sl m), M1; rep from * 2 more times, knit to end, M1—8 sts inc'd; 378 sts.

RND 4: Purl.

RND 5: With B, rep Rnd 3—386 sts.

RND 6: Purl.

RND 7: With A, Rep Rnd 3—394 sts.

RND 8: Purl.

RNDS 9–10: Rep Rnds 5–6—402 sts.

Second Edging

Note: This edging is worked with a dpn perpendicularly to the live sts. At each corner, work 3 rows before joining to corner wrap st at end of 4th row, then work 3 rows before joining to next live wrap st at end of foll 4th row.

ROW 1: With A and dpn, CO 7 sts.

ROW 2: K6, k2tog (last edge st and 1 wrap st). Notice that the wrap sts are a different color than the edging sts.

ROW 3: K3, yo, k4—8 sts.

ROW 4: K7, k2tog (last edge st and 1 wrap st).

ROW 5: K3, yo, k5—9 sts.

ROW 6: K8, k2tog (last edge st and 1 wrap st).

ROW 7: K3, yo, k6—10 sts.

ROW 8: K9, k2tog (last edge st and 1 wrap st).

ROW 9: K3, yo, k7—11 sts.

ROW 10: K10, k2tog (last edge st and 1 wrap st).

ROW 11 (BOBBLE ROW): K3, yo, k7, MB (see page 74).

ROW 12: BO 6 sts, k5, k2tog (last edge st and 1 wrap st)—6 sts rem.

ROW 13: K3, yo, k3—7 sts.

ROWS 14–24: Rep Rows 2–12 once.

Rep Rows 13–24 until all wrap sts have been used. BO rem sts. Cut yarn, leaving a 20" (51 cm) tail. Thread tail on a tapestry needle and sew CO edge to BO edge.

Weave in loose ends. Wet-block and pin to finished measurements. Let air-dry completely before removing pins.

shawls

◁▷

Shawls are my first love in the world of knit (and crochet) design. I think of a shawl as a two-dimensional canvas on which I can paint a story of texture, color, and geometric shapes. In this chapter, I wanted to really push the limits of knitting to incorporate some of the wonderful traits of crochet. Lelani (page 80) features knitted flower motifs that are joined in a similar fashion to crochet motifs. Serpentine (page 88) focuses on an edging that is very similar in construction to crochet's hairpin lace. The beaded edging of Tama (page 94) is worked by manipulating the yarn on the needles in the same fashion as crochet chain stitches. The swagged edging on Warrior Wings (page 98) is directly inspired by scalloped crochet edgings. The swirling vortex of knitted lace in Tide Pool (page 104) is my geometric expression of the naturally grown spiral.

lelani
FLOWER MOTIF SHAWL

This generously sized, luxurious shawl is an exquisite way to add warmth and drama to any outfit. The circular flower motifs that form the back are worked in rows and are joined to adjacent motifs as they are worked. Then stitches for the garter-stitch sides are picked up along the sides of the back panel and worked as large triangles simultaneously with a lacy edging. Wear this triangular shawl pinned, tied, or wrapped in the traditional methods, or lace the side triangles through the edges of the flower motifs on the opposite sides for a secure wrap that allows the edging to cascade down the front in beautiful drapes.

NOTES

- See the accompanying DVD for a demonstration on working the flower motifs.

MATERIALS

FINISHED SIZE
About 78" (198 cm) wide and 27" (68.5 cm) long.

YARN
DK weight (#3 Light).

shown here: Blue Sky Alpaca Melange (100% baby alpaca; 110 yd [100 m]/50 g): #800 Cornflower, 5 skeins.

NEEDLES
Size U.S. 3 (3.25 mm): straight plus 1 extra needle for three-needle bind-off. *Adjust needle size if necessary to obtain the correct gauge.*

NOTIONS
Contrasting cotton waste yarn for provisional cast-on; markers (m); tapestry needle.

GAUGE
16 stitches and 32 rows = 4" (10 cm) in garter stitch, after blocking. Each motif measures about 8¼" (21 cm) square, after blocking. Exact gauge is not critical for this project.

Motif 1

CO 12 sts.

ROW 1: Knit.

ROW 2: *K1 wrapping the yarn 4 times around the needle, k1; rep from *.

ROW 3: Sl all 12 sts to right-hand needle, dropping all extra loops, then sl these sts back to left-hand needle, then work (k1, yo, k1, yo, k1) in each st—60 sts.

ROW 4: Knit.

Edging

Note: The remainder of the motif is worked perpendicular to Row 4; the last st of every other row is knitted together with a live st from Row 4.

SET-UP ROW: With waste yarn and WS facing, use a provisional method (see Glossary) to CO 8 sts, turn, k7, k2tog (1 edging st and 1 st from Row 4 of motif).

ROW 1: K2, [yo, k2tog] 2 times, yo, k2—9 sts.

ROW 2: K2, yo, k2, [yo, k2tog] 2 times, k2tog (1 edging st and 1 st from Row 4 of motif)—10 sts.

ROW 3: K2, [yo, k2tog] 2 times, k2, yo, k2—11 sts.

ROW 4: K2, yo, k4, [yo, k2tog] 2 times, k2tog (1 edging st and 1 st from Row 4 of motif)—12 sts.

ROW 5: K2, [yo, k2tog] 2 times, k4, yo, k2—13 sts.

ROW 6: K2, yo, k6, [yo, k2tog] 2 times, k2tog (1 edging st and 1 st from Row 4 of motif)—14 sts.

ROW 7: K2, [yo, k2tog] 2 times, k6, yo, k2—15 sts.

ROW 8: K2, yo, k8, [yo, k2tog] 2 times, k2tog (1 edging st and 1 st from Row 4 of motif)—16 sts.

ROW 9: K2, [yo, k2tog] 2 times, k8, yo, k2—17 sts.

ROW 10: BO 10 sts (1 st on right-hand needle), k1, [yo, k2tog] 2 times, k1—7 sts rem.

ROW 11: K2, [yo, k2tog] 2 times, yo, k1f&b—9 sts.

ROWS 12–20: Rep Rows 2–10 once.

Rep Rows 11–20 ten more times.

NEXT ROW: Use the three-needle method (see Glossary) to BO the last row tog with the set-up row of the edging.

Thread CO tail on tapestry needle and sew tog Rows 1 and 2 to form a circle. Fasten off. Weave in loose ends.

Motif 2

Join first two petals of edging (indicated by blue and green dots on schematic) to Motif 1 at end of Edging Rows 9 and 19 as foll: Do not turn at end of row, insert right needle tip into tip of first petal of motif to be joined, yo and draw through loop—1 st. Turn work.

NEXT ROW: Sl 1, k1, psso, cont to BO 10 sts (1 st on right-hand needle), k1, [yo, k2tog] 2 times, k1—7 sts rem.

Join third petal (indicated by red dot on Construction Diagram) as foll: At end of next Edging Row 9, use the knitted method (see Glossary) to CO 4 sts, insert right needle tip in end of next petal, yo, and draw through loop, turn.

NEXT ROW: Sl 1, k1, psso, cont to BO 14 sts (the 4 new sts CO and the foll 10 sts; 1 st on right needle tip).

Note: This is the corner petal that will join four motifs in one point.

Work rem petals without joining.

When joining the next two motifs at the corner petal, CO 2 sts instead of 4, join with sl st in center of the same join st as for Motifs 1 and 2, BO 2 sts.

Work another corner join in the third join from the first corner join on Motifs 3 and 4.

Join Motif 5 to the corner join of Motifs 2, 3, and 4. Join Motif 6 to the corner join of Motifs 1, 2, and 5.

Construction Diagram

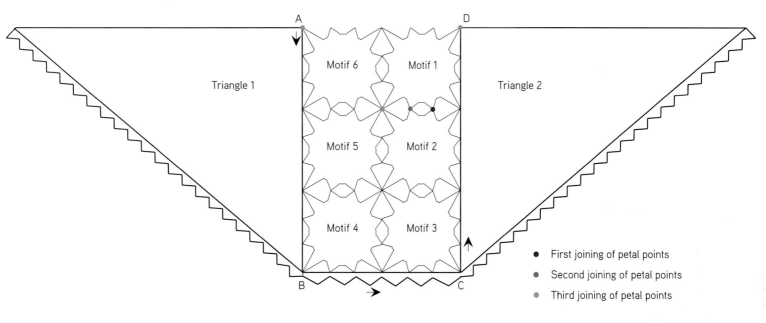

- ● First joining of petal points
- ● Second joining of petal points
- ● Third joining of petal points

This shawl is composed of 3 sections made up of 6 motifs, 2 triangles and edging.
Work each motif separately and join tips of petals as you work, beginning with Motif 2.

Triangle 1 is picked up beginning at A and working toward B, picking up stitches in the
petal points and casting on stitches between points. Edging stitches are cast on using knitted cast-on.

After completing Triangle 1, return to B and pick up and k8 sts in the 8 cast-on edging stitches
and work in the direction of the arrow toward C.

Triangle 2 is begun by picking up stitches in the petal points and casting on stitches between
points in the direction of the arrow toward D, in the same manner as for Triangle 1.

◂▸◂▸ *Once you get the feel for making and joining the flower motifs, why not make a full rectangular wrap or scarf exclusively in the flower motifs? Challenge your friends to guess if it is knitted or crocheted.*

Side Triangles

Note: The side triangles are worked sideways. Use a marker to visually separate each triangle from the edging. The decreases are worked next to the marker on every other row.

Triangle 1

Working along edge of motifs, pick up and knit 1 st in corner petal of top motif, *use the knitted method to CO 11 sts, pick up and knit 1 st in next petal; rep from * 8 more times (CO edge is joined to every petal), CO 8 more sts—117 sts total.

SET-UP ROW: K8, place marker (pm), knit to end.

ROW 1: Knit to 2 sts before m, k2tog, sl m, k2, [yo, k2tog] 2 times, yo, k2—117 sts; 108 sts rem before m, 9 sts after m.

ROW 2: K2, yo, k2, [yo, k2tog] 2 times, k1, sl m, knit to end—118 sts.

ROW 3: Knit to 2 sts before m, k2tog, sl m, k2, [yo, k2tog] 2 times, k2, yo, k2—118 sts; 107 sts rem before m, 11 sts after m.

ROW 4: K2, yo, k4, [yo, k2tog] 2 times, k1, sl m, knit to end—119 sts.

ROW 5: Knit to 2 sts before m, k2tog, sl m, k2, [yo, k2tog] 2 times, k4, yo, k2—119 sts; 106 sts rem before m, 13 sts after m.

ROW 6: K2, yo, k6, [yo, k2tog] 2 times, k1, sl m, knit to end—120 sts.

ROW 7: Knit to 2 sts before m, k2tog, sl m, k2, [yo, k2tog] 2 times, k6, yo, k2—120 sts; 105 sts rem before m, 15 sts after m.

ROW 8: K2, yo, k8, [yo, k2tog] 2 times, k2tog, k1, sl m, knit to end—121 sts.

ROW 9: Knit to 2 sts before m, k2tog, sl m, k2, [yo, k2tog] 2 times, k8, yo, k2—121 sts; 104 sts rem before m, 17 sts after m.

ROW 10: BO 10 sts (1 st on right-hand needle), k1, [yo, k2tog] 2 times, k1, sl m, knit to end—111 sts; 7 sts before m, 104 sts after m.

ROW 11: Knit to 2 sts before m, k2tog, sl m, k2, [yo, k2tog] 2 times, yo, k1f&b (see Glossary)—112 sts; 103 sts before m; 9 sts after m.

ROWS 12–20: Rep Rows 2–10 once—108 sts; 99 sts before m, 9 sts after m.

Rep Rows 11–20 nineteen more times, then rep Rows 11–16 once more—15 sts rem; piece measures about 30" (76 cm) from pick-up row.

NEXT ROW: K2tog, removing m, k1, [yo, k2tog] 2 times, k6, yo, k2—15 sts.

NEXT ROW: K2, yo, k8, [yo, k2tog] 2 times, k1—16 sts.

NEXT ROW: K2, [yo, k2tog] 2 times, k8, yo, k2—17 sts.

NEXT ROW: BO 10 sts (1 st on right-hand needle), k1, [yo, k2tog] 2 times, k1—7 sts rem. Loosely BO all sts.

Center Edging

Note: This edging begins from the CO edge of Triangle 1. It is worked alone along the bottom of the center motifs and is joined to the points of the center motifs at the end of every Row 10 as foll:

With RS facing, pick up and k8 in 8 sts CO at end of first triangle, turn.

ROW 1: K2, [yo, k2tog] 2 times, yo, k2—9 sts.

ROW 2: K2, yo, k2, [yo, k2tog] 2 times, k1—10 sts.

ROW 3: K2, [yo, k2tog] 2 times, k2, yo, k2—11 sts.

ROW 4: K2, yo, k4, [yo, k2tog] 2 times, k1—12 sts.

ROW 5: K2, [yo, k2tog] 2 times, k4, yo, k2—13 sts.

ROW 6: K2, yo, k6, [yo, k2tog] 2 times, k1—14 sts.

ROW 7: K2, [yo, k2tog] 2 times, k6, yo, k2—15 sts.

ROW 8: K2, yo, k8, [yo, k2tog] 2 times, k1—16 sts.

ROW 9: Inset tip of right-hand needle into end of motif petal, k2, [yo, k2tog] 2 times, k8, yo, k2—17 sts and tip of petal.

ROW 10: BO 10 sts (1 st on right-hand needle), k1, [yo, k2tog] 2 times, k2tog (1 edging st and tip of petal)—7 sts rem.

ROW 11: K2, [yo, k2tog] 2 times, yo, k1f&b—9 sts.

ROWS 12–20: Rep Rows 2–10 once.

Rep Rows 11–20 four more times.

Triangle 2

SET-UP ROW: At the end of the last rep of Row 10, pm, pick up and knit 1 st in corner petal (last petal joined on center edging), *use the knitted method to CO 11 sts, pick up and knit 1 st in next petal (along the vertical edge of the center motifs; see Construction Diagram); rep from * 8 more times (CO edge is joined to every petal along vertical edge of center motifs)—117 sts total.

ROW 1: Knit to 2 sts before m, k2tog, sl m, k2, [yo, k2tog] 2 times, yo, k2—117 sts; 108 sts rem before m, 9 sts after m.

ROW 2: K2, yo, k2, [yo, k2tog] 2 times, k1, sl m, knit to end—118 sts.

ROW 3: Knit to 2 sts before m, k2tog, sl m, k2, [yo, k2tog] 2 times, k2, yo, k2—118 sts; 107 sts rem before m, 11 sts after m.

ROW 4: K2, yo, k4, [yo, k2tog] 2 times, k1, sl m, knit to end—119 sts.

ROW 5: Knit to 2 sts before m, k2tog, sl m, k2, [yo, k2tog] 2 times, k4, yo, k2—119 sts; 106 sts rem before m, 13 sts after m.

ROW 6: K2, yo, k6, [yo, k2tog] 2 times, k1, sl m, knit to end—120 sts.

ROW 7: Knit to 2 sts before m, k2tog, sl m, k2, [yo, k2tog] 2 times, k6, yo, k2—120 sts; 105 sts rem before m, 15 sts after m.

ROW 8: K2, yo, k8, [yo, k2tog] 2 times, k2tog, k1, sl m, knit to end—121 sts.

ROW 9: Knit to 2 sts before m, k2tog, sl m, k2, [yo, k2tog] 2 times, k8, yo, k2—121 sts; 104 sts rem before m, 17 sts after m.

ROW 10: BO 10 sts (1 st on right-hand needle), k1, [yo, k2tog] 2 times, k1, sl m, knit to end—111 sts; 7 sts before m, 104 sts after m.

ROW 11: Knit to 2 sts before m, k2tog, sl m, k2, [yo, k2tog] 2 times, yo, k1f&b—112 sts; 103 sts before m, 9 sts after m.

ROWS 12–20: Rep Rows 2–10 once—108 sts; 99 sts before m, 9 sts after m.

Rep Rows 11–20 nineteen more times, then rep Rows 11–16 once more—15 sts rem; piece measures about 30" (76 cm) from CO edge.

NEXT ROW: K2tog, removing m, k1, [yo, k2tog] 2 times, k6, yo, k2—15 sts.

NEXT ROW: K2, yo, k8, [yo, k2tog] 2 times, k1—16 sts.

NEXT ROW: K2, [yo, k2tog] 2 times, k8, yo, k2—17 sts.

NEXT ROW: BO 10 sts (1 st on right-hand needle), k1, [yo, k2tog] 2 times, k1—7 sts rem.

Loosely BO all sts.

Finishing

Weave in loose ends. Wet-block and pin to finished measurements. Let air-dry completely before removing pins.

serpentine
REVERSIBLE SHAWLETTE

Worked from the top down in garter stitch and shaped with simple yarnover increases, this shawlette is both reversible and incredibly easy to knit. The edging is worked by knitting strips that are decreased along one side to give a look similar to crochet hairpin lace. You may find the edging a little tricky at first, but it can become quite addictive, and the result is well worth the effort! Tie this shawl around your shoulders on a cool evening or wrap it twice around your neck to show off an abundance of serpentine ruffles.

NOTES

- If you prefer a simpler look, substitute the picot edging used in the Lucky Clover Scarf (page 20), the chain-stitch edging used in the Tama Shawlette (page 94), or the really loose bind-off used in the Melange Scarf (page 26).

- See the accompanying DVD for a demonstration on working the serpentine edging.

MATERIALS

FINISHED SIZE
About 20½" (52 cm) wide and 48" (122 cm) long.

YARN
Sportweight (#2 Fine).

shown here: Blue Sky Alpacas Alpaca Silk (50% alpaca, 50% silk; 146 yd [133 m]/50 g): #129 Amethyst, 3 skeins.

NEEDLES
Size U.S. 4 (3.5 mm): 24" (60 cm) circular (cir) and 1 double-pointed (dpn). *Adjust needle size if necessary to obtain the correct gauge.*

NOTIONS
Tapestry needle.

GAUGE
14 stitches and 32 rows = 4" (10 cm) in garter stitch, after blocking.

Serpentine Edging

The serpentine edging reminds me of individual rose petals delicately sewn to the edge of the otherwise simple shawl. The shawl pattern is easy to repeat and could be continued for several more inches before beginning the edging—just be sure to have the right number of stitches to allow for full 5-stitch repeats of the edging. This edging could be applied to all sorts of projects, including skirts, capes, dresses, tunics, and blankets.

Keep in mind that the right side of the shawl is always facing up as the edging is worked. When turning the edge stitches back and forth while working them in rows, alternate the direction of turning every row so the working yarn doesn't get twisted in the fabric.

Note: This edging is worked perpendicularly along the lower edge of shawl in strips that involve 7 sts: 3 sts at the beg of the strip, 3 sts used for a modified three-needle BO, and 1 st returned to the left needle tip (along with the rest of the shawl sts).

ROW 1: Beg with the first 3 shawl sts, yo, k1, k1f&b (see Glossary), [yo] 2 times (counts as 1 st), k1—6 sts.

ROW 2: [Yo] 2 times, k2tog (dropping second loop of double yo from previous row), k4.

ROW 3: [Yo] 2 times, k2tog, k4 (dropping second loop of double yo from previous row).

Rep Row 3 until there are 13 loops on each side of the strip.

BO AS FOLL: Hold work with the shawl on your left, the edging on your right, and the tips of the needles pointing toward opposite sides. With dpn, pick up each of the 13 loops along the edge closest to the live shawl sts one at a time from back to front, just putting the loops on the needle, not picking them up and knitting them (**Figure 1**). With right needle tip, *pass second loop over first loop and off the needle; rep from * 11 more times—1 loop st rem on dpn (**Figure 2**). Place this st on right needle tip and pass live strip st over this loop, pull working yarn to tighten, then return last st to right needle tip (**Figure 3**)—6 sts on right needle tip (counting double yo as 1 st). Turn right needle around and place on top of left needle so that RS are facing tog and both needle tips point to the right (**Figure 4**). Holding both needles parallel, [insert tip of dpn into first 2 strip sts (as if to k2tog) on the front needle and into the first shawl st on the back needle (**Figure 5**), and

knit these 3 sts tog] 2 times, then pass first st over second st and off the needle—1 st BO. Insert tip of dpn into next 2 strip sts (as if to k2tog) while dropping second loop of double yo, and into the next shawl st on and knit these 3 sts tog. Pass the first st over the second st and off the needle—1 st rem (**Figure 6**). Return this st to left needle tip.

Repeat from Row 1 for each serpentine shell.

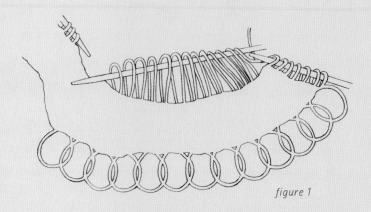

figure 1

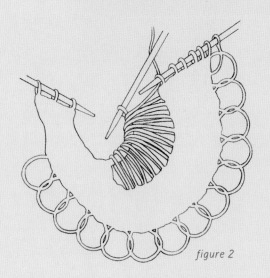

figure 2

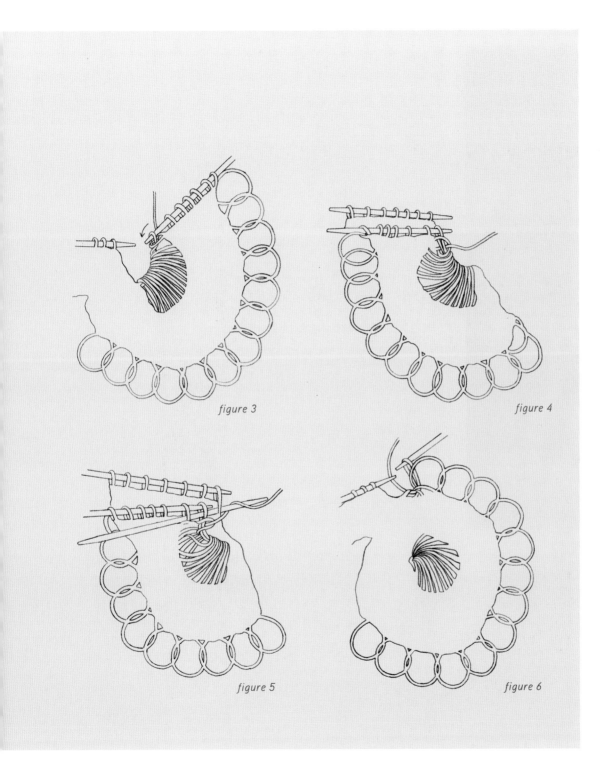

figure 3

figure 4

figure 5

figure 6

I designed this simple garter-stitch shawl to learn how to make the serpentine edging, which reminds me of individual rose petals. Once you learn the edging, you could apply it to the hems of all types of projects, such as skirts, capes, dresses, tunics, and blankets.

Shawl

CO 5 sts.

ROW 1: K1, *yo, k1; rep from *—9 sts.

ROW 2 AND ALL EVEN-NUMBERED ROWS: Knit.

ROW 3: K1, yo, k3, yo, k1, yo, k3, yo, k1—13 sts.

ROW 5: K1, yo, k5, yo, k1, yo, k5, yo, k1—17 sts.

ROW 7: K1, yo, k7, yo, k1, yo, k7, yo, k1—21 sts.

ROW 9: K1, yo, k9, yo, k1, yo, k9, yo, k1—25 sts.

ROW 11: K1, yo, 11, yo, k1, yo, k11, yo, k1—29 sts.

Cont in this manner, inc 4 sts every odd-numbered row until there are 197 sts—piece measures about 17" (43 cm) from CO, measured along the center.

NEXT ROW: K1, yo, k1, [yo, k2tog] 48 times, yo, k1, yo, [k2tog, yo] 48 times, k1, yo, k1—201 sts.

NEXT ROW: K1, yo, k99, yo, k1, yo, k99, yo, k1—205 sts.

Edging

Work serpentine edging as described on page 90, rep the edging for every 5 sts on the needle.

Finishing

Weave in loose ends. Wet-block and pin to finished measurements. Let air-dry completely before removing pins.

tama
BEAD-TRIMMED
SEASHELL SHAWLETTE

When I first began to knit, I fell in love with the way the increases and decreases in the feather-and-fan pattern—one of the oldest lace patterns—create the look of rippling waves. For this shawl, I modified the traditional pattern to create vertical panels of waves that are separated by narrow garter-stitch panels. Each wave panel increases from a few stitches at the neck to a full cresting wave at the hem. For a bit of shimmer, I added five beads evenly spaced along the lower edge of each wave and a crochet-inspired "chain 7" at the lower edge of each garter-stitch panel.

NOTES

- See the accompanying DVD for a demonstration on working the chain bind-off.

MATERIALS

FINISHED SIZE
About 52" (132 cm) wide and 24" (61 cm) long.

YARN
Sportweight (#2 Fine).

shown here: Wagtail Yarns 4-Ply 100% Fine Kid Mohair (100% kid mohair; 410 yd [375 m]/100 g): #710 025 Burnt Sienna, 2 skeins.

NEEDLES
Size U.S. 7 (4.5 mm): 24" (60 cm) circular (cir). *Adjust needle size if necessary to obtain the correct gauge.*

NOTIONS
139 round size 6° seed beads (shown in Toho Bead's silver-lined Rosaline beads); fine needle for threading beads on yarn; tapestry needle.

GAUGE
16 stitches and 20 rows = 4" (10 cm) in garter stitch, after blocking.

Shawl

CO 4 sts. Knit 20 rows. Cont as foll:

ROW 1: K4, turn piece 90 degrees, pick up and knit 10 sts along selvedge edge, turn piece 90 degrees again, pick up and knit 4 sts along CO edge—18 sts total.

ROWS 2, 4, AND 6: Knit.

ROW 3: K4, [k1f&b (see Glossary)] 10 times, k4—28 sts.

ROW 5: K4, [k1f&b] 20 times, k4—48 sts.

ROW 7: K4, *(k1, yo, k1) in space before next st, k4; rep from *—81 sts.

ROW 8: K4, *p3, k4; rep from *.

ROWS 9 AND 10: Knit.

Work Rows 1–28 of Tama chart, then rep Rows 25–28 six more times, then work Rows 29–52, then rep Rows 49–52 four more times—367 sts. Knit 6 rows even. Cut yarn.

Thread 139 beads onto yarn, then work a modification of the chain BO (see page 28) as foll: K2tog, [push bead snugly up to last st on right-hand needle, yo, insert left-hand needle into second st, pass it over the yo and off the needle] 7 times, k2tog, pass st over, *BO 4 sts, [push bead snugly up to last st on right-hand needle, yo, insert left-hand needle into second st, pass it over the yo and off the needle, BO 5 sts] 5 times, k2tog, [push bead snugly up to last st on right-hand needle, yo, insert left-hand needle into second st, pass it over the yo and off the needle] 7 times, k2tog, pass st over; rep from * 10 more times. Fasten off last st.

Finishing

Wet-block and pin to finished measurements. Let air-dry completely before removing pins. Weave in loose ends.

Tama

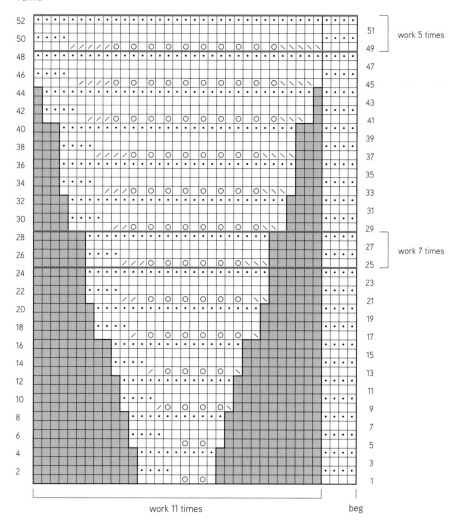

work 5 times

work 7 times

work 11 times   beg

- ☐ k on RS; p on WS
- • p on RS; k on WS
- ○ yo
- ╱ k2tog
- ╲ ssk
- ▨ no stitch
- ▬ pattern repeat

By nature, the half-circle shape sits nicely on the shoulders without pinning or tying. The beaded trim is elegant and sophisticated when matched to the color of the yarn. For a more dramatic look, add sparkly contrasting beads.

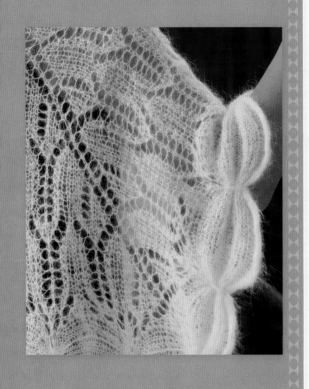

warrior wings
CINCHED-EDGE SHAWL

Because the ethereal halo of the brushed alpaca yarn in this shawl makes me think of angel wings, I wanted to create a lace-stitch pattern that resembled layers of feathers. Coupled with the strong alpaca fiber in the yarn, this shawl represents a mythological creature's shield—it appears to be soft and airy but is empowered with the strength of a warrior's shield. The simple 18-row repeat in the stitch pattern gives the illusion of motifs that are offset brick-fashion. The edging is added by working perpendicularly to the live stitches on the last row of the shawl and is cinched at regular intervals to create the pretty scallops.

NOTES

- This shawl is worked from the top down, beginning with a short rectangle from which the shawl stitches are picked up.

- When placing stitch markers, use one color to separate the selvedge edge from the three lace sections; use a second color to separate the increase sections from each lace section. The second set of markers is removed at the end of each 18-row repeat, then replaced at the beginning of the next repeat.

- See the accompanying DVD for a demonstration on working the wrapped stitches in the swag at the lower edge.

MATERIALS

FINISHED SIZE
About 57" (145 cm) wide and 22" (56 cm) long.

YARN
DK weight (#3 Light).

shown here: Alpaca Yarn Company Halo (100% brushed suri alpaca; 514 yd [470 m]/50 g): #7010 Wings, 2 balls.

NEEDLES
Size U.S. 6 (4.0 mm): 24" (60 cm) circular (cir). *Adjust needle size if necessary to obtain the correct gauge.*

NOTIONS
Smooth, cotton waste yarn for provisional cast-on; markers (m; 2 sets in contrast color or design); tapestry needle.

GAUGE
16 stitches and 24 rows = 4" (10 cm) in lace pattern, after blocking.

Shawl

With waste yarn, use a provisional method (see Glossary) to CO 8 sts. Do not join.
Knit 30 rows.

Shawl Set-Up

ROW 1: K8, place marker (pm), pick up and knit 15 sts along selvedge edge, pm, k8—31 sts.

ROW 2: Knit.

ROW 3: K8, slip marker (sl m), [k1, yo] 15 times, sl m, k8—46 sts.

ROW 4: Knit.

Shawl Body

Knitting the first 8 and the last 8 sts of every row, work center sts (beg with 30 sts) according to Rows 1–18 of Lace chart—100 sts. Rep Rows 1–18 four more times—316 sts.

Lace

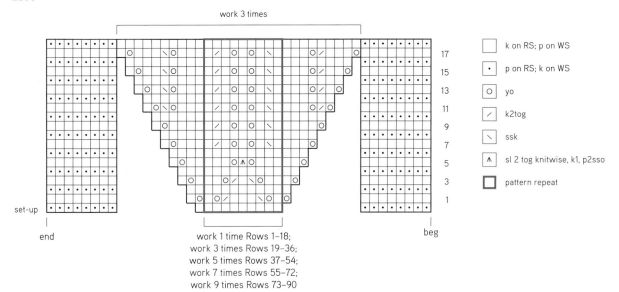

	k on RS; p on WS
•	p on RS; k on WS
O	yo
/	k2tog
\	ssk
⋏	sl 2 tog knitwise, k1, p2sso
☐	pattern repeat

work 3 times

set-up

end

work 1 time Rows 1–18;
work 3 times Rows 19–36;
work 5 times Rows 37–54;
work 7 times Rows 55–72;
work 9 times Rows 73–90

beg

The beautiful swagged edging on this ◀▶◀▶◀ shawl is deceptively easy to knit. Try adding it to the neckline, cuff, or hem of a sweater.

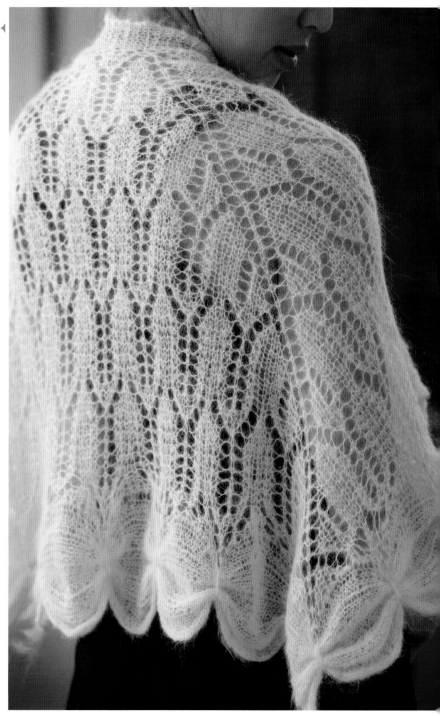

Construction Diagram

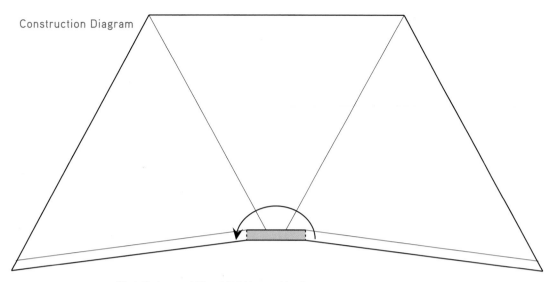

Work first row of Shawl Set-Up, working in
direction of the arrow, by knitting 8 stitches
on the needle, pick up and knit 15 stitches
along one long edge of selvedge, then
knit 8 stitches from invisible cast-on.

Finishing

Edging

Using the knitted method (see Glossary), CO 24
sts to the end of the 316 sts on needle—340 sts
total.

ROW 1: [K4, p4] 2 times, k4, p3, p2tog (1 edge st
and 1 shawl st)—1 shawl st dec'd.

ROW 2: [K4, p4] 3 times.

Rep Rows 1 and 2 eleven more times—24 rows
total; 12 shawl sts dec'd.

SWAG ROW: Sl 24 sts individually to right needle
tip, wrap working yarn 3 times around these 24
sts and pull yarn to cinch the sts to 2" (5 cm)
wide, then return these sts to left needle tip.
Rep from Row 1 until all shawl sts have been
used, omitting the swag row on the last group
of sts. Loosely BO all sts.

Weave in loose ends. Wet-block and pin to
finished measurements. Let air-dry completely
before removing pins.

tide pool
SPIRAL LACE SHAWL

Imagine the swirls of rushing water flowing in and out of a tide pool, to the rhythm of the crashing ocean waves, and you've got the inspiration for this airy shawl. The spiral design is created by picking up and knitting a series of triangles that grow in three concentric rings. Each edge of the finished piece is bordered with a simple garter-stitch lace pattern. This type of large square can be worn in a number of ways—open and generously wrapped around, the top third folded over for a shawl collar for a rectangular wrap, folded in half for a smaller rectangular shape, or folded in half on the diagonal for a triangular shape.

- Each section is picked up and knitted from the end of the previous section; take care to pick up stitches neatly and evenly.

- To space stitches evenly when picking up along long edges, use removable markers to divide the length into four equal quarters.

- See the accompanying DVD for a demonstration on working the yarnover bind-off.

MATERIALS

FINISHED SIZE
About 55" (139.5 cm) square.

YARN
Laceweight (#0 Lace).

shown here: Webs Valley Yarn 2/14 Alpaca Silk (80% alpaca, 20% silk; 1,736 yd [1,587 m]/8 oz cone): Pacific, 850 yd [777 m] or 3.9 oz.

NEEDLES
Size U.S. 7 (4.5 mm): 24" and 32" (60 and 80 cm) circular (cir). *Adjust needle size if necessary to obtain the correct gauge.*

NOTIONS
Removable markers (m); tapestry needle.

GAUGE
12 stitches and 22 rows = 4" (10 cm) in lace pattern; 16 stitches and 26 rows = 4" (10 cm) in garter stitch, after blocking.
Note: This fabric is very stretchy; exact gauge is not critical.

Center Square

CO 40 sts.

ROW 1: K20, [yo, k2tog] 10 times.

ROW 2: [Yo, k2tog] 10 times, k20.

ROWS 3–20: Rep Rows 1 and 2 nine more times—20 rows total.

ROW 21: [Yo, k2tog] 10 times, k20.

ROW 22: K20, [yo, k2tog] 10 times.

ROWS 23–40: Rep Rows 21 and 22 nine more times—piece measures about 8" (20.5 cm) from CO.

Level 1 Triangles

Triangle 1A

ROW 1: *Yo, k2tog; rep from *—40 sts.

ROW 2: Yo, k4tog, *yo, k2tog; rep from * to end of row—2 sts dec'd.

Rep Row 2 until 6 sts rem.

NEXT ROW: Yo, k4tog, yo, k2tog—4 sts rem.

NEXT ROW: Yo, k4tog—2 sts rem.

NEXT ROW: K2tog—1 st rem.

Fasten off.

Triangle 1B

With RS facing, pick up and knit 40 sts along selvedge edge of center square.

DEC ROW: K3tog, knit to end—2 sts dec'd.

Rep dec row until 2 sts rem.

NEXT ROW: K2tog—1 st rem.

Fasten off.

Triangle 1C

With RS facing, pick up and knit 40 sts along CO edge of center square.

Work Rows 2–21 of Triangle 1A—1 st rem. Fasten off.

Yarnover Bind-Off

The yarnover bind-off is extremely elastic and allows you to block and stretch the lace shawl without any restriction from the bind-off edge. It is my favorite standard bind-off for knitted lace.

K1, *yo, k1 (**Figure 1**), then lift the yo and the first st over the second st and off the needle (**Figure 2**) to BO 1 st; rep from * for desired number of sts.

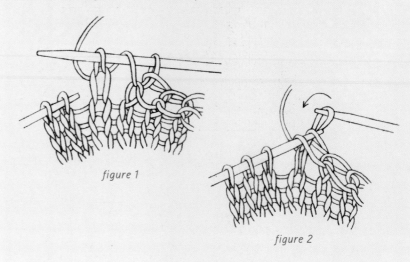

figure 1

figure 2

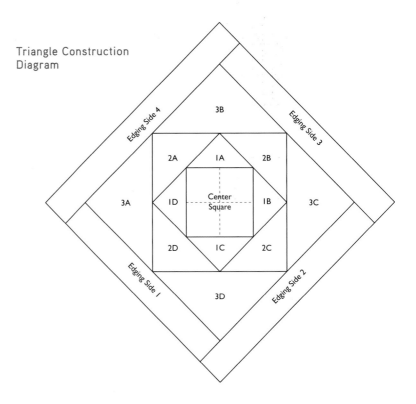

Triangle Construction Diagram

Triangles 1A and 1C

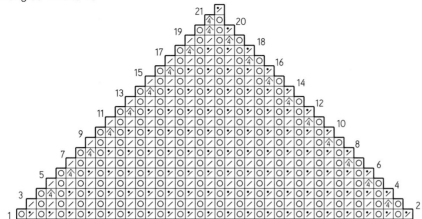

Triangles 1B and 1D

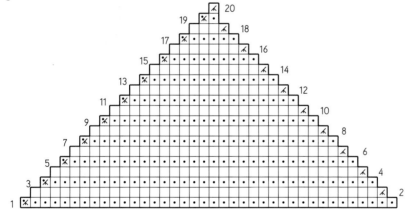

Center Square

work 10 times

work 10 times

	k on RS; p on WS			k3tog on RS
	p on RS; k on WS			k3tog on WS
	yo			k4tog on RS; k4tog on WS
	k2tog on RS			pattern repeat
	k2tog on WS			

Triangle 1D

With RS facing, pick up and knit 40 sts along other edge of center square. Work as for Triangle 1B.

Level 2 Triangles

Triangle 2A

With RS facing and using removable markers to help space the sts evenly (see Notes), pick up and knit 20 st each along edge of Triangles 1A and 1D—40 sts total.

ROW 1: K2tog, *yo, k2tog; rep from *—1 st dec'd.

ROW 2: K2tog, *yo, k2tog; rep from * to last st, k1—1 st dec'd.

ROW 3: Yo, k3tog, *yo, k2tog; rep from * to last st, k1—1 st dec'd.

ROW 4: Yo, k3tog, *yo, k2tog; rep from *—1 st dec'd; 36 sts rem.

Rep Rows 1–4 until 1 st rem. Fasten off.

Triangle 2B

With RS facing, pick up and knit 20 sts each along edge of Triangles 1B and 1A—40 sts total.

DEC ROW: K2tog, knit to end—1 st dec'd.

Rep dec row until 1 st rem. Fasten off.

Triangle 2C

With RS facing, pick up and knit 20 sts each along edge of Triangles 1C and 1B—40 sts total. Work as for Triangle 2A.

Triangle 2D

With RS facing, pick up and knit 20 sts each along edge of Triangles 1D and 1C—40 sts total. Work as for Triangle 2B.

Level 3 Triangles

Triangle 3A

With RS facing and using removable markers to help space the sts evenly, pick up and knit 40 sts each along edge of Triangles 2A and 2D—80 sts total.

ROW 1: K2tog, *yo, k2tog; rep from *—1 st dec'd.

ROW 2: K2tog, *yo, k2tog; rep from * to last st, k1—1 st dec'd.

ROW 3: Yo, k3tog, *yo, k2tog; rep from * to last st, k1—1 st dec'd.

ROW 4: Yo, k3tog, *yo, k2tog; rep from * to last st—1 st dec'd; 76 sts rem.

Rep Rows 1–4 until 1 st rem. Fasten off.

Triangle 3B

With RS facing, pick up and knit 40 sts each along edge of Triangles 2B and 2A—80 sts total.

DEC ROW: K2tog, knit to end—1 st dec'd.

Rep dec row until 1 st rem. Fasten off.

Triangle 3C

With RS facing, pick up and knit 40 sts each along edge of Triangles 2C and 2B—80 sts total. Work as for Triangle 3A.

Triangle 3D

With RS facing, pick up and knit 40 sts each along edge of Triangles 2D and 2C—80 sts total. Work as for Triangle 3B.

Finishing

Edging

Note: The edging is worked separately on all four sides, log cabin style; not all at once in the rnd. The first side of the edging is picked up from the shawl edge only. The second side of the edging is picked up from the shawl edge and the short edge of the first edging. The third side of the edging is picked up from the shawl edge and the short edge of the second edging. The fourth side of the edging is picked up from the short edge on the third side of edging, the shawl edge, and the rem short edge on the first side of edging.

◄ ► ◄ ► *To keep a consistent look throughout the shawl, be sure to always pick up stitches along the edges of triangles the same way.*

Edging

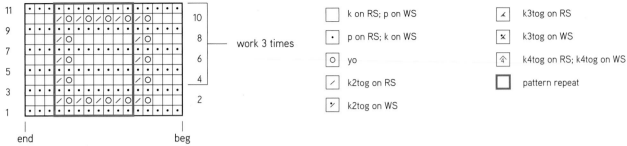

Legend:

- ⬜ k on RS; p on WS
- • p on RS; k on WS
- O yo
- ╱ k2tog on RS
- ⅄ k2tog on WS
- �╱ k3tog on RS
- ⋉ k3tog on WS
- ⬆ k4tog on RS; k4tog on WS
- ⬛ pattern repeat

First Side

With RS facing, pick up and knit 80 sts each along edge of Triangles 3A and 3D—160 sts total. Work according to Edging chart as foll:

ROW 1: (WS) Knit.

ROW 2: (RS) K3, *yo, k2tog; rep from * to last 3 sts, k3.

ROWS 3, 5, 7, AND 9: Knit.

ROWS 4, 6, AND 8: K3, yo, k2tog, *k6, yo, k2tog; rep from * to last 3 sts, k3.

ROW 10: Rep Row 2.

ROW 11: Rep Row 3.

Rep Rows 4–11 two more times, then knit 2 rows.

Use the yarnover method (see page 106) to BO all sts.

Second Side

With RS facing, pick up and knit 24 sts along short edge of edging on first side and 80 sts each along edge of Triangles 3D and 3C—184 sts total. Work as for first side.

Third Side

With RS facing, pick up and knit 24 sts along short edge of second side and 80 sts each along edge of Triangles 3C and 3B—184 sts total. Work as for first side.

Fourth Side

With RS facing, pick up and knit 24 sts along short edge of third side, 80 sts each along edge of Triangles 3B and 3A, and 24 sts along short edge of first side—208 sts total. Work as for first side.

Weave in loose ends. Wet-block and pin to finished measurements. Let air-dry completely before removing pins.

skirts

◀▶

At its simplest, a skirt can be a draped garment made from a simple piece of cloth. For added texture and drama, fitting a skirt to the waist and creating shaping to the hips and beyond requires some of the skills you may already possess from shaping yokes in sweaters. For Flamenco (page 114), I used a round yoke sweater formula to create the shaping through the hips. The ruffles are added onto the fabric in an incredibly easy technique that requires no sewing. The volume in Arcelia (page 120) is created with a couple of larger pleats just below the waist. Both skirts can be worn in a number of ways—Arcelia can even be worn as a top!

flamenco
RUFFLED DRAWSTRING SKIRT

Can't you just imagine dancing the night away in this hip-hugging, swishing, ruffled-hem drawstring skirt? It's knitted from the top down and shaped with concentric increases along the way. A generous mass of tight ruffles worked with a sequined yarn adds drama near the short ruffle around the hem. The ruffles are picked up along strategically placed ridges and can be worn on either the right or left side, the front, or the back of the skirt. The drawstring holes are evenly placed around the waistband—just adjust the placement of the drawstring tie to position the ruffles where you want.

NOTES

- Every sixth round of lower skirt has a section of purled stitches that create a ridge from which to pick up and knit the ruffles.

- See the accompanying DVD for a demonstration of picking up and knitting stitches for the ruffles.

MATERIALS

FINISHED SIZE
About 30 (32¾, 36, 38¾)" (76 [83, 91.5, 98.5] cm) waist circumference, 37½ (41, 45, 48¼)" (95 [104, 114.5, 122.5] cm) hip circumference, and 45 (49, 54, 58)" (114.5 [124.5, 137, 147.5] cm) hem ruffle circumference above the hem ruffle. Skirt shown measures 37½" (95 cm) at hips.

YARN
Sportweight (#2 Fine).

shown here: Tilli Tomas Pure & Simple (100% spun silk; 260 yd [283 m]/100 g): Ruby Wine (MC), 5 (5, 6, 6) skeins. Tilli Tomas Disco Lights (90% spun silk, 10% petite sequins; 225 yd [206 m]/100 g): Ruby Wine (CC), 2 (2, 2, 2) skeins.

NEEDLES
Size U.S. 6 (4 mm): 32" (80 cm) circular (cir) and set of 2 double-pointed (dpn). *Adjust needle size if necessary to obtain the correct gauge.*

NOTIONS
Markers (m); tapestry needle.

GAUGE
24 stitches and 30 rows = 4" (10 cm) in stockinette stitch, worked in rounds.

Skirt

With MC, CO 180 (196, 216, 232) sts.

JOINING RND: *K2, p2; rep from * to end of row, place marker (pm), and join for working in rnds, being careful not to twist sts.

Work in rib as established (knit the knits and purl the purls) for 4 rnds.

EYELET RND: *Yo, k2tog, yo, p2tog; rep from *.

Work in rib as established for 6 more rnds—piece measures about 1¾" (4.5 cm) from CO. Work even in St st until piece measures 2" (5 cm) from last row of rib.

INC RND 1: *K3, inc 1 by knitting into the st in the row below the first st on the left needle, k1; rep from *—225 (245, 270, 290) sts.

Work even in St st until piece measures 7" (18 cm) from last row of rib.

INC RND 2: *K4, inc 1 by knitting into the st in the row below the first st on the left needle, k1; rep from *—270 (294, 324, 348) sts.

Work even in St st until piece measures 14" (35.5 cm) from last row of rib.

NEXT RND: K126 (138, 153, 165), p18 to denote placement of first ruffle, k126 (138, 153, 165).

Knit 5 rnds.

NEXT RND: K120 (132, 147, 159), p30 to denote placement of second ruffle, k120 (132, 147, 159).

Knit 5 rnds.

NEXT RND: K114 (126, 141, 153), p42 to denote placement of third ruffle, k114 (126, 141, 153).

Knit 5 rnds.

NEXT RND: K108 (120, 135, 147), p54 to denote placement of fourth ruffle, k108 (120, 135, 147).

Knit 5 rnds.

NEXT RND: K102 (114, 129, 141), p66 to denote placement of fifth ruffle, k102 (114, 129, 141).

Knit 5 rnds.

NEXT RND: K96 (108, 123, 135), p78 to denote

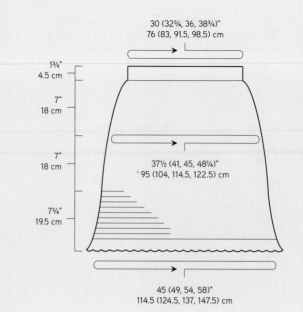

30 (32¾, 36, 38¾)"
76 (83, 91.5, 98.5) cm

1¾"
4.5 cm

7"
18 cm

37½ (41, 45, 48¼)"
95 (104, 114.5, 122.5) cm

7"
18 cm

7¾"
19.5 cm

45 (49, 54, 58)"
114.5 (124.5, 137, 147.5) cm

◄ ► ◄ ► *The deep red of this skirt is bold and adventurous. For a more modest bridal look, substitute white or ivory yarn. For cocktail or eveningwear, try black yarn with sequins!*

placement of sixth ruffle, k96 (108, 123, 135).

Knit 5 rnds.

NEXT RND: K90 (102, 117, 129), p90 to denote placement of seventh ruffle, k90 (102, 117, 129).

Knit 5 rnds.

NEXT RND: k84 (96, 111, 123), p102 to denote placement of eighth ruffle, k84 (96, 111, 123).

Knit 5 rnds.

Rep the last 6 rnds once more. Work even until piece measures 22" (56 cm) from last row of rib (9 ruffles total).

Edging

RND 1: Purl.

RND 2: *Yo, k1; rep from *—540 (588, 648, 696) sts.

RND 3: Purl.

RND 4: Knit.

RND 5: Purl.

Rep the last two rnds until ruffle measures 1½" (3.8 cm) long. Use the yarnover method (see page 106) to loosely BO as foll: K1, *yo, k1, insert left needle tip in first knit st and yo, then lift both off the needle—1 st rem on right needle tip; rep from * until 1 st rem. Fasten off.

Ruffles

With CC and RS facing, pick up and knit 18 sts along first section of purl ridges. Knit every row until ruffle measures 1½" (3.8 cm) from pick-up row. Loosely BO as for edging.

Repeat for rem 8 ruffles, picking up 30, 42, 54, 66, 78, 90, 102, and 102 sts respectively.

I-Cord

With MC and dpn, CO 4 sts. Work I-cord (see Glossary) until piece measures 57 (60, 63, 66)" (145 [152.5, 160, 167.5] cm) or desired length from CO.

NEXT ROW: Sl 1, k2tog, psso—1 st rem.

Cut yarn and pull tail through rem st to secure.

Finishing

Weave in loose ends. Wet-block and pin to finished measurements. Let air-dry completely before removing pins.

Beg and end at desired starting point for center front, thread I-cord through eyelets at waistband.

arcelia
GYPSY WRAP SKIRT

Have you ever seen a gypsy dancing in a colorful flowing skirt that jingles with coins or beads sewn onto the hem? The circle lace hem on this casual skirt reminds me of a free-spirited international traveler. It has a very simple lace pattern that will pop dramatically over a contrasting skirt or dress. For a dressier Eastern-inspired look, wear it as a halter top over a tunic and leggings. The pattern includes a couple of unusual techniques, including pleats, crochet-inspired circular motif edging, and an incredibly quick openwork pattern. The edging is worked vertically but joined in two different ways for the hem and side of the skirt.

NOTES

- The lower edging is worked first. After the skirt is complete, stitches are picked up along the vertical side edge and the side edging is joined to the skirt as it is worked.

- The body stitches are bound off tightly in a method similar to the standard bind-off, but every other stitch is worked as k2tog.

- See the accompanying DVD for a demonstration on working the circle lace edging.

MATERIALS

FINISHED SIZE
About 42 (46½)" (106.5 [118] cm) wide, unwrapped. To fit 30 (34)" (76 [86.5] cm) waist.

YARN
DK weight (#3 Light).

shown here: Stitch Diva's Studio Silk (100% silk; 120 yd [110 m]/50 g): Shrinking Violet, 5 (6) skeins.

NEEDLES
Size U.S. 6 (4 mm): 32" (80 cm) circular (cir) and set of double pointed (dpn) for making pleats. *Adjust needle size if necessary to obtain the correct gauge.*

NOTIONS
Tapestry needle.

GAUGE
18½ stitches and 15 rows = 4" (10 cm) in lace pattern, after blocking.

Lower Medallion Edging

WITH DPN, CO 3 sts. Do not join.

ROW 1: (RS) K1f&b (see Glossary), yo, k2—5 sts.

ROWS 2, 4, 6, 8, AND 10: Knit.

ROW 3: K2, yo, k1, yo, k2—7 sts.

ROW 5: K2, yo, k3, yo, k2—9 sts.

ROW 7: K1, ssk, yo, sl 2, k1, p2sso, yo, k2tog, k1—7 sts rem.

ROW 9: K1, ssk, yo, k3tog, k1—5 sts rem.

ROW 11: Ssk, k1, k2tog—3 sts rem.

ROW 12: K3tog—1 st rem.

ROW 13: Knit into the front, back, and front of the same st—3 sts.

ROW 14: Rep Row 2.

Rep Rows 1–14 until there are 26 (28) circle motifs, ending with Row 12. Fasten off.

16-Stitch Pleat

Pleats add interesting depth and texture to otherwise two-dimensional knitted fabric. As long as you choose a large multiple of six stitches (for the front, middle, and back of each side), you could modify the pleats to any size.

Slip 16 sts onto dpn for underlay, sl next 16 sts onto another dpn for fold-under. With WS facing tog, hold fold-under behind left needle tip, then, with RS tog, hold underlay behind fold-under—3 needles held tog at left of work. *Insert right needle tip into first st on all 3 left needle tips and knit these sts tog—1 st on right needle; rep from * to end of pleat sts.

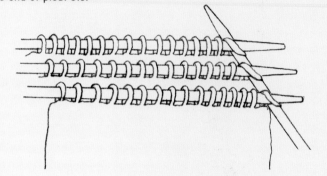

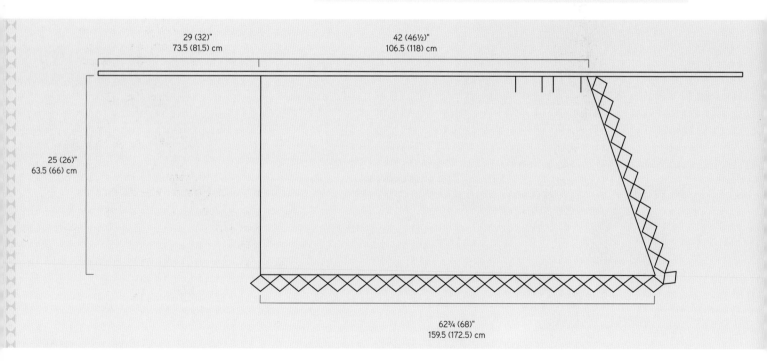

◄ ► ◄ ► *Turn this skirt into a wrap simply by omitting the pleats and waistband. Work the circle motifs around all four edges for a full-frame border of medallion lace.*

Skirt

Note: Skip the first motif when picking up sts for the skirt. This skipped motif will be picked up for the vertical edge of motifs along the sides of the finished skirt.

With cir needle and RS facing, pick up and knit 2 sts evenly spaced along top edge of second motif from the edge. *Use the knitted method (see Glossary) to CO 9 sts, pick up and knit 3 sts evenly along top edge of next motif; rep from * 22 (24) more times, CO 9 sts, then on the last motif, pick up and knit 2 sts evenly spaced—289 (313) sts total.

ROW 1: (WS) K1, *k2, pass second st on right needle tip over first st, k1, pass second st on right needle tip over first st, sl 1 pwise with yarn in back (wyb), pass second st on right needle tip over first st (3 sts BO); rep from *—73 (79) sts rem.

ROW 2: K1, *yo, k1; rep from *—145 (157) sts.

ROW 3: Knit.

ROW 4: K1, *k1 in the yo space below, k2; rep from *—217 (235) sts.

ROW 5: K1, *k1, in the same yo space below, k3; rep from *, ending last rep k2—289 (313) sts.

Rep Rows 1–5 until piece measures 25 (26)" (63.5 [66] cm) from pick-up row, ending with Row 5 of patt.

PLEAT ROW: *K4 (8), work 16-st pleat (see box on page 122) over next 48 sts (32 sts dec'd); rep from * once, knit to end, then use the knitted method to CO 88 (96) sts for waistband tie—313 (345) sts.

NEXT ROW: Knit to end, then use the knitted method to CO 88 (96) more sts for waistband tie—401 (441) sts.

Knit 5 rows even.

NEXT ROW: Loosely BO 88 (96) sts, then tightly BO the 225 (249) center body sts as foll: k2tog, *k1, pass second over first st and off needle, k2tog, pass the second st over first st and off needle; rep from * until center 225 (249) sts are BO, k88 (96)—88 (96) sts rem.

Loosely BO rem sts.

Finishing

Weave in loose ends. Wet-block and pin to finished measurements. Let air-dry completely before removing pins.

Side Edging

With dpn and WS facing, (pick up and knit 1 st, yo, pick up and knit 1 st) in top corner (the corner pointing up toward the waistband) of the rem free motif at the lower edge—3 sts.

Turn, k3.

ROW 1: K1f&b, yo, k2—5 sts.

ROWS 2 AND 4: Knit.

ROW 3: K2, yo, k1, yo, k2—7 sts.

ROW 5: K2, yo, k3, yo, k2—9 sts.

ROW 6: K8, insert left needle tip in edge of second rep along side edge of skirt, knit this edge tog with last st.

ROW 7: K1, ssk, yo, sl 2, k1, p2sso, yo, k2tog, k1—7 sts rem.

ROWS 8 AND 10: Knit.

ROW 9: K1, ssk, yo, k3tog, k1—5 sts rem.

ROW 11: Ssk, k1, k2tog—3 sts rem.

ROW 12: K3tog—1 st rem.

ROW 13: Knit into the front, back, and front of the same stitch—3 sts.

ROW 14: Knit.

Rep Rows 1–14, joining each Row 6 with about every other rep of lace pattern along side edge and ending with Row 12—1 st rem. Fasten off last st, leaving a long tail. Sew top of last motif to waist tie.

glossary

Abbreviations

beg	begin(s); beginning	p	purl	tbl	through back loop
BO	bind off	p1f&b	purl into front and back of same stitch	tog	together
CC	contrast color			WS	wrong side
cm	centimeter(s)	patt(s)	pattern(s)	wyb	with yarn in back
cn	cable needle	psso	pass slipped stitch over	wyf	with yarn in front
CO	cast on	pwise	purlwise, as if to purl	yd	yard(s)
cont	continue(s); continuing	rem	remain(s); remaining	yo	yarnover
dec(s)	decrease(s); decreasing	rep	repeat(s); repeating	*	repeat starting point
dpn	double-pointed needles	rev St st	reverse stockinette stitch	( )	alternate measurements and/or instructions
foll	follow(s); following	rnd(s)	round(s)		
g	gram(s)	RS	right side	[ ]	work instructions as a group a specified number of times
inc(s)	increase(s); increasing	sl	slip		
k	knit	sl st	slip st (slip 1 stitch purlwise unless otherwise indicated)		
k1f&b	knit into the front and back of same stitch	ssk	slip 2 stitches knitwise, one at a time, from the left needle to right needle, insert left needle tip through both front loops and knit together from this position (1 stitch decrease)		
kwise	knitwise, as if to knit				
m	marker(s)				
MC	main color	st	stitch(es)		
mm	millimeter(s)	St st	stockinette stitch		
M1	make one (increase)				

Bind-Offs

Standard Bind-Off

Knit the first stitch, *knit the next stitch (2 stitches on right needle), insert left needle tip into first stitch on right needle (**Figure 1**) and lift this stitch up and over the second stitch (**Figure 2**) and off the needle (**Figure 3**). Repeat from * for the desired number of stitches.

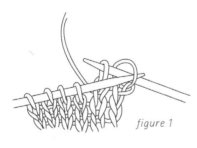

figure 1

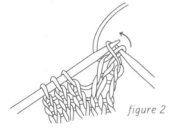

figure 2

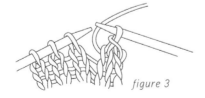

figure 3

Three-Needle Bind-Off

Place the stitches to be joined onto two separate needles and hold the needles parallel so that the right sides of knitting face together. Insert a third needle into the first stitch on each of the other two needles (**Figure 1**) and knit them together as one stitch (**Figure 2**), *knit the next stitch on each needle the same way, then use one of the left needle tips to lift the first stitch over the second and off the needle (**Figure 3**). Repeat from * until no stitches remain on first two needles. Cut yarn and pull tail through last stitch to secure.

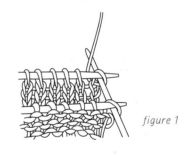

figure 1

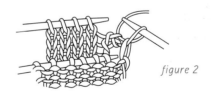

figure 2

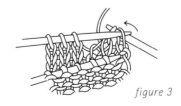

figure 3

Cast-Ons

Invisible Provisional Cast-On

Make a loose slipknot of working yarn and place it on the right needle. Hold a length of contrasting waste yarn next to the slipknot and around your left thumb; hold working yarn over your left index finger. *Bring the right needle forward under the waste yarn, over the working yarn, grab a loop of working yarn (**Figure 1**), then bring the needle back behind the working yarn to grab a second loop (**Figure 2**). Repeat from * for the desired number of stitches. When you're ready to work in the opposite direction, place the exposed loops on a knitting needle as you pull out the waste yarn.

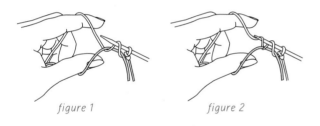

figure 1   *figure 2*

Knitted Cast-On

Make a slipknot of working yarn and place it on the left needle if there are no stitches already there. *Use the right needle to knit the first stitch (or slipknot) on left needle (**Figure 1**) and place new loop onto left needle to form a new stitch (**Figure 2**). Repeat from * for the desired number of stitches, always working into the last stitch made.

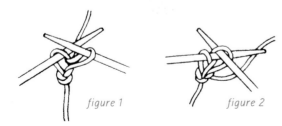

figure 1   *figure 2*

Long-Tail Cast-On

Leaving a long tail (about ½" [1.3 cm] for each stitch to be cast on), make a slipknot and place on right needle. Place thumb and index finger of your left hand between the yarn ends so that working yarn is around your index finger and tail end is around your thumb and secure the yarn ends with your other fingers. Hold your palm upward, making a V of yarn (**Figure 1**). *Bring needle up through loop on thumb (**Figure 2**), catch first strand around index finger, and go back down through loop on thumb (**Figure 3**). Drop loop off thumb and, placing thumb back in V configuration, tighten resulting stitch on needle (**Figure 4**). Repeat from * for the desired number of stitches.

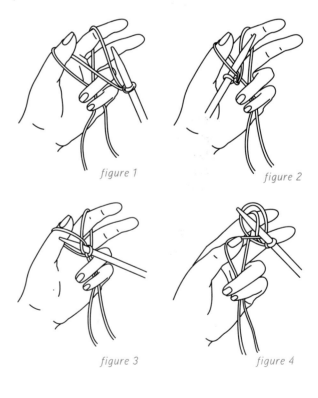

figure 1   *figure 2*

figure 3   *figure 4*

Embroidery
Chain Stitch

Bring threaded needle out from back to front, form a short loop, then insert needle back in where it came out. Keeping the loop under the needle, bring the needle back out a short distance to the right.

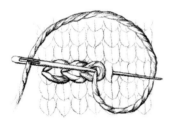

I-Cord (also called Knit-Cord)

Using two double-pointed needles, cast on the desired number of stitches (usually 3 to 4). *Without turning the needle, slide stitches to other end of needle, pull the yarn around the back, and knit the stitches as usual. Repeat from * for desired length.

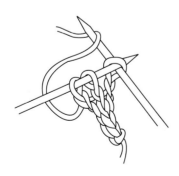

Increases
Bar Increase Knitwise (k1f&b)

Knit into a stitch but leave it on the left needle (**Figure 1**), then knit through the back loop of the same stitch (**Figure 2**) and slip the original stitch off the needle (**Figure 3**).

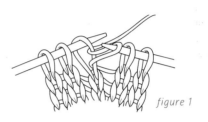

figure 1

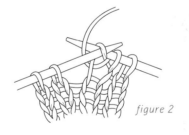

figure 2

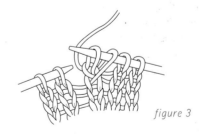

figure 3

Bar Increase Purlwise (p1f&b)

Purl into a stitch but leave the stitch on the left needle (**Figure 1**), then purl through the back loop of the same stitch (**Figure 2**) and slip the original stitch off the needle.

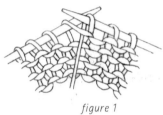

figure 1

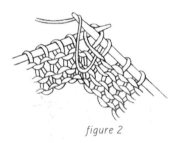

figure 2

Lifted Increase

Note: If no slant direction is specified, use the right slant.

Right Slant (LRI)

Knit into the back of the stitch (in the "purl bump") in the row directly below the stitch on the needle (**Figure 1**), then knit the stitch on the needle (**Figure 2**), and slip the original stitch off the needle.

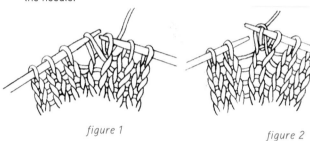

figure 1   *figure 2*

Left Slant (LLI)

Insert left needle tip into the back of the stitch below the stitch just knitted (**Figure 1**), then knit this stitch (**Figure 2**).

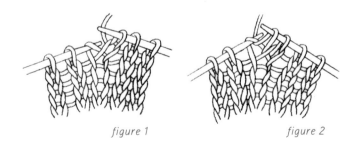

figure 1   *figure 2*

Raised Make-One (M1)

Note: Use the left slant if no direction of slant is specified.

Left Slant (M1L)

With left needle tip, lift the strand between the last knitted stitch and the first stitch on the left needle from front to back (Figure 1), then knit the lifted loop through the back (**Figure 2**).

figure 1

figure 2

Right Slant (M1R)

With left needle tip, lift the strand between the needles from back to front (**Figure 1**), then knit the lifted loop through the front (**Figure 2**).

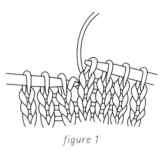

figure 1

figure 2

Pick Up and Purl

Pick Up and Purl

With wrong side of work facing and working from right to left, *insert needle tip under selvedge stitch from the far side to the near side **(Figure 1)**, wrap yarn around needle, and pull a loop through **(Figure 2)**. Repeat from * for desired number of stitches.

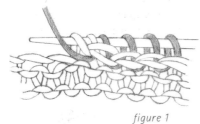

figure 1

figure 2

Mattress Stitch

Place the pieces to be seamed on a table, right sides facing up. Begin at the lower edge and work upward as follows for your stitch pattern:

Stockinette Stitch with 1-Stitch Seam Allowance

Insert threaded needle under one bar between the 2 edge stitches on one piece, then under the corresponding bar plus the bar above it on the other piece **(Figure 1)**. *Pick up the next two bars on the first piece **(Figure 2)**, then the next two bars on the other **(Figure 3)**. Repeat from *, ending by picking up the last bar or pair of bars on the first piece.

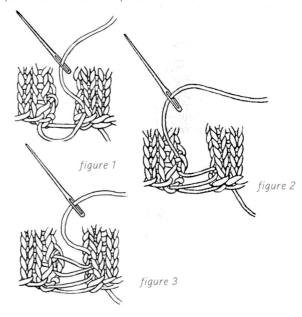

figure 1

figure 2

figure 3

Stockinette Stitch with ½-Stitch Seam Allowance

To reduce bulk in the mattress-stitch seam, work as for the 1-stitch seam allowance but pick up the bars in the center of the edge stitches instead of between the last 2 stitches.

Short-Rows
Short-Rows Knit Side

Work to turning point, slip next stitch purlwise (**Figure 1**), bring the yarn to the front, then slip the same stitch back to the left needle (**Figure 2**), turn the work around and bring the yarn in position for the next stitch—1 stitch has been wrapped and the yarn is correctly positioned to work the next stitch. When you come to a wrapped stitch on a subsequent row, hide the wrap by working it together with the wrapped stitch as follows: Insert right needle tip under the wrap (from the front if wrapped stitch is a knit stitch; from the back if wrapped stitch is a purl stitch; Figure 3), then into the stitch on the needle, and work the stitch and its wrap together as a single stitch.

Short-Rows Purl Side

Work to the turning point, slip the next stitch purlwise to the right needle, bring the yarn to the back of the work (**Figure 1**), return the slipped stitch to the left needle, bring the yarn to the front between the needles (**Figure 2**), and turn the work so that the knit side is facing—1 stitch has been wrapped and the yarn is correctly positioned to knit the next stitch. To hide the wrap on a subsequent purl row, work to the wrapped stitch, use the tip of the right needle to pick up the wrap from the back, place it on the left needle (**Figure 3**), then purl it together with the wrapped stitch.

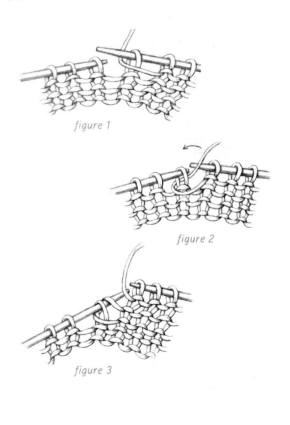

figure 1

figure 2

figure 3

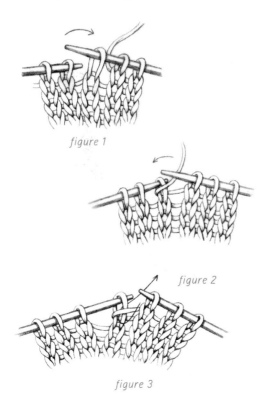

figure 1

figure 2

figure 3

resources

Books

Epstein, Nicky. *Knitting on the Edge.* New York: Sixth & Spring, 2004.

Kinzel, Marianne. *First Book of Modern Lace Knitting.* Mineola, New York: Dover, 1972.

Walker, Barbara G. *A Treasury of Knitting Patterns.* Pittsville, Wisconsin: Schoolhouse Press, 1998.

———. *A Second Treasury of Knitting Patterns.* Pittsville, Wisconsin: Schoolhouse Press, 1998.

———. *A Third Treasury of Knitting Patterns.* Pittsville, Wisconsin: Schoolhouse Press, 1998.

———. *A Fourth Treasury of Knitting Patterns.* Pittsville, Wisconsin: Schoolhouse Press, 1998.

———. *Knitting From The Top Down.* Pittsville, Wisconsin: Schoolhouse Press, 1996.

Yarn

Alpaca Yarn Company
144 Roosevelt Ave., Bay #1
York, PA 17401
thealpacayarnco.com

Bijou Basin Ranch
PO Box 154
Elbert, CO 80106
bijoubasinranch.com

Blue Sky Alpacas
PO Box 88
Cedar, MN 55011
blueskyalpacas.com

Buffalo Gold
PO Box 516
11316 CR 604
Burleson, TX 76097
buffalogold.net

Green Mountain Spinnery
PO Box 568
Putney, VT 05346
spinnery.com

Lantern Moon
7911 N.E. 33rd Dr., Ste. 140
Portland, OR 97211
lanternmoon.com

Louet North America
3425 Hands Rd.
Prescott, ON
Canada K0E 1T0
louet.com

Malabrigo
malabrigoyarn.com

Stitch Diva Studios
stitchdiva.com

Tahki Stacy Charles/ Filatura Di Crosa/Collezione
70-30 80th St., Bldg. 36
Ridgewood, NY 11385
tahkistacycharles.com

Tilli Tomas
tillitomas.com

Valley Yarns
WEBS-America's Yarn Store
75 Service Center Rd.
Northampton, MA 01060
yarn.com

Wagtail Yarns
731 Buxton Rd.
Childers
Queensland 4660
Australia
wagtailyarns.com